Across the Centuries

Teaching Units for Timeless Children's Literature
from a Christian Perspective

Level D
Volume 2

Authors: Annette Rose and Jan Gillette

The Sign of the Beaver ❧ *From the Mixed-Up Files . . .*
Blue Willow ❧ *Call It Courage*

Across the Centuries: Level D: Volume 2

Created and Developed by
Christian Academic Publications and Services, Inc.

Managing Editor	Sharon R. Berry, Ph.D.
Project Editor	Barry M. Morris, Ph.D.
Authors	Annette Rose
	Jan Gillette
Illustrators	Barbara Crowe
	Lance Lot Studios
Production	Sherry Berry
	Sandy Kilgo

Published by
LifeWay Christian School Resources
127 Ninth Avenue North
Nashville, TN 37234-0182
1-800-458-2772
www.lifeway.com

All Rights Reserved
Copyright © 1999 LifeWay™

ISBN: 0-7673-9432-1
Dewey Decimal Classification: 372.64
Subject Heading: LITERATURE – – TEXTS

CONTENTS

Preface 4

The Sign of the Beaver
    Introduction 5
    Instructional Plan 7
    Enrichment 26
    Masters 27

From the Mixed-Up Files of Mrs. Basil E. Frankweiler
    Introduction 47
    Instructional Plan 49
    Enrichment 72
    Masters 75

Blue Willow
    Introduction 93
    Instructional Plan 97
    Enrichment 110
    Masters 113

Call It Courage
    Introduction 139
    Instructional Plan 143
    Enrichment 155
    Masters 157

Welcome to *Across the Centuries*, a series of teaching units for timeless children's literature from a Christian perspective. The volume you are using is one of many available for students in various grade levels.

> Level A — Preschool and Kindergarten
> Level B — First and Second Grades
> Level C — Third and Fourth Grades
> Level D — Fifth and Sixth Grades
> Level E — Seventh and Eighth Grades
> Level F — High School

In this series, books of exceptional literary quality serve as the basis for instructional units developed by gifted classroom teachers focusing on creative, proven techniques to engage and challenge students. Additionally, natural opportunities were taken to integrate each book with Biblical principles and a Christian worldview that incorporates character building aimed toward high ethical values.

The series provides unique resources for teachers and parents who want to convey a Christian perspective of life to their children and teens. Each volume contains four to five instructional units that present clear directions for teaching a unit from the introduction to instructional strategies to questions and answers to evaluation and conclusion. Masters designed for duplication present student exercises, vocabulary studies, background information, research projects, craft ideas and assessment instruments. In addition, masters provide the teacher with instructional materials and patterns. All masters are designed with art and graphic components to make them visually appealing to students. Answer keys appear in the text in conjunction with the teaching strategies. Each unit contains suggestions for enrichment including class activities, research methods, projects, field trips, crafts and summary experiences.

All materials are highly flexible and teachers are encouraged to select those activities which best suit the interests of their students and the time they have available. A unit can easily be implemented as a class project, as an optional, enrichment activity or as a challenge to only one or two students. The time devoted to instruction can thus vary from a full class period over several weeks to minimal interaction as students independently develop portfolios. Teachers can use all or part of a unit as they design and implement their instructional programs based on their knowledge of their classes. The materials are especially useful to parents in homeschooling or as enrichment to their regular school programs.

To achieve optimal success in teaching the units in this volume, begin by selecting a book that complements your curriculum. Read the entire unit and review all the masters and suggested activities. Based on the level and interests of your students and the time to be devoted to the material, plan your instructional program. Choose the activities, strategies and projects that best complement your goals. Prepare materials and copy masters in advance. Contact special guests and initiate any related projects through parent volunteers. Implement your plan and enjoy the results.

May you be blessed as you teach these selections of award-winning literature in relation to the wonderful words and works of God.

THE SIGN OF THE BEAVER
by Elizabeth George Speare

INTRODUCTION

The Sign of the Beaver tells the story of two young boys from very different backgrounds. Matt Hallowell is a twelve-year-old left alone in the wilderness to protect the new family home while his father brings his mother and sister from Quincy, Massachusetts. Attean is a young Native American boy who lost his parents in the French and Indian War. The author draws her readers into the story as these boys slowly develop a friendship in which both of them must examine their own prejudices. As students read the book, they will examine their own feelings about people of different cultures and discover how they formed their opinions.

OBJECTIVES:

1. Students will discern that God promises they will never be alone.

2. Students will develop knowledge of the locations on a map of North America.

3. Students will locate the routes to the frontier taken by pioneers during the colonial period.

4. Students will demonstrate a knowledge of life in a colonial settlement.

5. Students will compare and contrast the Native American culture of Attean with the pioneer culture of Matt and his family.

6. Students will list facts about bees, their habitats, and the process of making honey.

7. Students will discern what qualities are desirable in a friend.

SUMMARY OF STORY:

Matt Hallowell, a twelve-year-old boy, has been left alone in the wilderness of Maine to guard the new log house and small corn fields he helped his father to prepare. His father has returned to Quincy, Massachusetts, to bring his mother and sister to their new family home. When Matt is injured by a swarm of bees, he is rescued and nursed back to health by Saknis, a tribal chief, and his grandson,

Attean, who is the same age as Matt. Both boys are hesitant to trust each other due to experiences and prejudices passed through the generations of their cultures. They cautiously begin a friendship based on mutual respect and the bond of young boys approaching manhood. They learn that, in spite of their cultural differences, both have strong family ties and a desire to live in peace.

ABOUT THE AUTHOR:

Elizabeth George Speare was born in Melrose, Massachusetts, in 1908. As a child, she wrote stories in a notebook that she kept with her most of the time. Upon graduating from college, she taught high school English in Massachusetts. Speare's historical fiction books are meticulously researched for authenticity. Her character development is unsurpassed among historical fiction authors. In 1989 Elizabeth George Speare won the Laura Ingalls Wilder Award for her body of work. She died in 1994.

Other books written by Elizabeth George Speare:

Life in Colonial America
Published by Random House, New York

The Witch of Blackbird Pond
Calico Captive
The Bronze Bow
Published by Houghton Mifflin, Boston

INSTRUCTIONAL PLAN

PREPARATION FOR READING: The following activities are designed to prepare your class for the study of *The Sign of the Beaver*.

1 Read *Robinson Crusoe* to the class far in advance of this novel study. Knowledge of this story will assist them in understanding the attitudes of both boys.

2 Write the word "wilderness" on the board. Ask students to write any thoughts the word brings to their mind. Discuss what they wrote and lead the discussion to thoughts of being alone for seven or more weeks in the wilderness. Discuss the basic needs for survival and how they could be met. Brainstorm with questions such as:

1) How would you know when the seven weeks had passed?
2) How would you react if a stranger wandered into your camp?
3) Suppose you had only one gun for hunting food and it was lost or stolen. What would you do for food?
4) After weeks of eating the same things, what would you long to eat the most?

3 Research the construction of a log cabin and let students volunteer to build a model out of building materials such as Lincoln Logs, craft sticks and paper rolls.

4 Take a field trip to an outdoor learning center. Arrange to have the guide discuss trail marking, telling directions in the wilderness, plant identification for harmful as well as helpful plants, and what to do if you were on a camping or hiking trip. If a field trip is not practical, invite a guest speaker, such as an Eagle Scout or Boy Scout leader, to come to the class to discuss these subjects.

5 Discuss the elements of a good adventure/survival story: suspense, excitement, obstacles faced by the protagonist. Write an adventure/survival story together as a class. Allow one student to put the story on chart paper as students dictate. Critique the story together. When you are comfortable with their understanding of this writing style, ask each student to write a creative adventure/survival story. Take class time for the stories to be read aloud. Students should peer edit each other's stories before presenting them to the class.

6 Pre-teach the new vocabulary students may encounter.

Lesson 1—Chapter 1: reckon, surveyor, puncheon, daub, chink, blunderbuss, matchlock, ruefully

Lesson 2—Chapters 2–4: proprietor, solitary, deacon, quaver, passel, begrudge, mite, salvage

Lesson 3—Chapters 5–7: boggy, wrenched, incomprehensible, defiance, glowered, finicky

Lesson 4—Chapters 8–10: scorn, adz, splice, stout, nonchalant, contemptuous, ponder

Lesson 5—Chapters 11–14: disdain, chagrin, indignant, goad, shrewd, improvise, inspiration

Lesson 6—Chapters 15–17: nimbly, falter, pungent, contortions, ramshackle, wampum

Lesson 7—Chapters 18–22: trespasser, placid, menace, intricate, wielded, manitou

Lesson 8—Chapters 23–25: meager, beseeching, prowess, gingerly, scant, lustrous, despised, typhus, aught

7 Implement one or more of these vocabulary activities at the beginning of each lesson.

1) Discuss the suffixes "er" and "or" and their meanings. Look up the definition of "survey" and "trespass" in a classroom dictionary.

Survey—to define boundaries of a section of land by measuring, using specifically designed tools

Trespass—to intrude unlawfully upon the property or rights of another

"Er" and "or" are often used as suffixes to change a verb into a noun. The newly formed noun tells who or what actually performed the verb.

Therefore, a surveyor is one who measures specific areas of land with specialized instruments to define its boundaries.

A trespasser is one who intrudes unlawfully on the property or rights of others.

Master 1.1 may be used for further practice using "er" and "or" to change verbs into nouns.

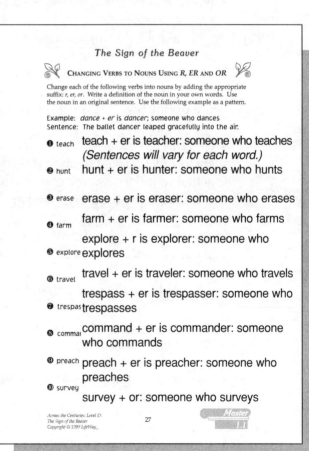

Across the Centuries: Level D
The Sign of the Beaver

2) Add vocabulary words from the current lesson in the novel to the current spelling list being studied.

3) Use a thesaurus to find a synonym for selected vocabulary words.

4) Before reading a lesson, allow students to skim the chapters and highlight or list the unfamiliar words they find. Allow individual students to attempt to define a word by using context clues. Verify meanings in a dictionary as needed.

5) Using large index cards, instruct each student to make vocabulary flash cards for each lesson. Write the word boldly with a marker on the front of each card. Write the definition lightly in pencil on the back. Use the flash cards for individual study or to play games to assist in learning the spelling and definitions of the words.

8) Discuss the work involved in planning, planting and maintaining a productive vegetable garden. Have the class list the steps: select a site, determine how the soil is turned and enriched, select the seeds, determine the best time for planting, etc.

Lesson 1 (Chapter 1)

1 After describing the feeling of being totally alone, instruct students to draw a picture of themselves lost in the wilderness.

2 Introduce the vocabulary for Lesson 1 and implement a vocabulary activity.

3 As Chapter 1 of *The Sign of the Beaver* is read, instruct students to write words or phrases that indicate Matt is alone in an uncomfortable environment. (Possibilities might be: edge of the clearing, father is gone, really alone, miles of wilderness on all sides, so quiet, cleared land. Accept reasonable interpretations.) After reading Chapter 1, discuss students' answers.

4 Find passages in the chapter to verify that Matt was uneasy about being alone. Instruct students to look up Isaiah 41:9–10 in their Bibles.

> Isaiah 41:9a–10 (NIV): I took you from the ends of the earth, from its farthest corners I called you. So do not fear, for I am with you; do not be dismayed, for I am your God. I will strengthen you and help you; I will uphold you with My righteous right hand.

Discuss how these verses could have been a source of comfort for Matt.

5 Read Psalm 23 together in unison and discuss the promises God makes. Instruct the students to write a letter to Matt interpreting what God wants him to know from Psalm 23. **Master 1.2** may be used for this purpose.

6 Gain permission to prepare a plot of ground and plant a garden of vegetables such as corn and pumpkins. Assign daily tasks to maintain the garden, reminding students that Matt had to take care of his family's garden all alone so they would have food supplies in the winter. To give students a sense of Matt's responsibilities, have them carry water in buckets for the garden. Discuss the following questions:

1) How many trips does it take back and forth from the water supply to water the garden sufficiently?
2) Does it have to be done every day?
3) Do weeds grow quickly?

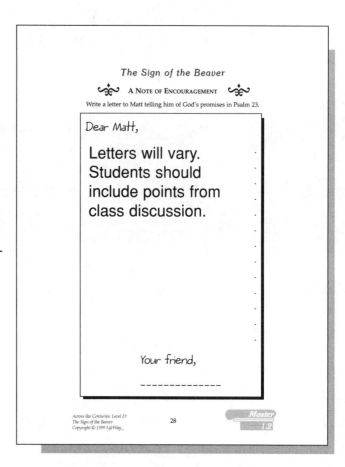

Across the Centuries: Level D
The Sign of the Beaver

Copyright © 1999 LifeWay

4) How often must the garden be weeded?
5) Matt had no pesticides, so what are some ways to control pests in your class garden?
6) What is the best way to fertilize your garden?

Students should begin to realize how hard Matt had to work each day just to have food to eat.

7 As an evaluation tool, direct students to write a paragraph explaining why the 23rd Psalm would be of great comfort to Matt. (Paragraph points should include some of the following: the Lord's leading us like lost lambs, His constant provision for our needs, His peace, His comfort, His protection from that which would harm us, His promise to us of a dwelling place with Him for eternity. Accept any points that support previous class discussion of Psalm 23.)

LESSON 2 (CHAPTERS 2-4)

1. Quickly review vocabulary from Lesson 1. Allow students to work with a partner to challenge each other's knowledge of the definitions and spelling. Make vocabulary flash cards for Lesson 2.

2. Read the last half of the first page of Chapter 3 together, beginning with the second paragraph. After reading the physical description of the character introduced, ask students to predict his personality.

3. Read Chapters 2-4. Ask students to note ways the author builds suspense in this section of the story: dark shadows moving, Matt waiting with muscles tensed, stranger approaching cabin, very deliberately looking the place over.

4. Discuss why the loss of his gun left Matt in a desperate situation. *(He now had no protection. He had no way to hunt for meat.)*

5. The guns of that era were called muskets. Muskets were long barreled rifles that used ignited gunpowder to traject the ammunition toward the target. Some muskets were matchlocks and some were flintlocks. Select two groups and instruct each group to research and illustrate the assigned weapon. Allow each group to show its illustration and explain how the specified firing mechanism worked. *(Matchlock: A slow-burning cord ignited to set off the charge. Flintlock: A flint located in the hammer struck a spark to set off the charge.)*

6. Provide students with the recipe for hasty pudding on **Master 2.1**. Instruct them to decorate around the recipe and use their imagination to illustrate as if it were a recipe card. They can cut out the recipe and glue it to a large index card. As a class, research and collect other colonial recipes and put them on index cards in the same way. Make copies of the collected recipes for each student so they can develop a collection of colonial recipes. Choose some of the dishes to make and serve in class. Invite another class or parents to share what has been made.

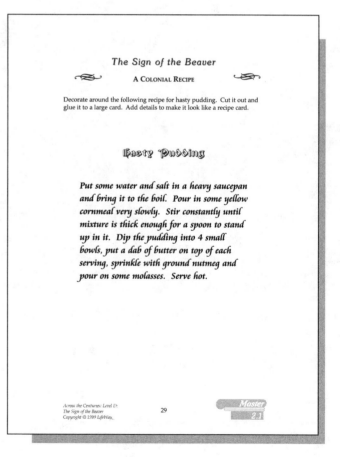

7 Distribute the colonial map on **Master 2.2** instructing students to label the specified tribes in their appropriate locations. Locate Massachusetts and point out that the Maine territory was actually part of Massachusetts at that time in history. Re-read in Chapter 1 the steps taken by Matt and his father to arrive at the land they had chosen to be their new home.

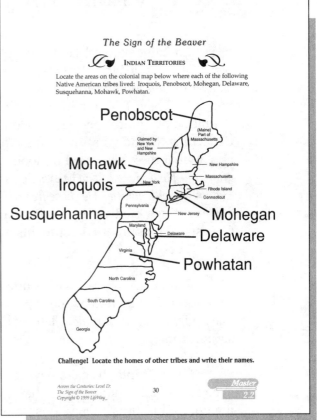

Brainstorm some ideas about what they would have to purchase to take with them. They would only be able to transport the absolute essentials to set up their new home. Locate the Penobscot River and try to determine the route they traveled. Brainstorm ideas about what it must have been like for Mother and Sarah, who were left behind. Point out that they were not left in the wilderness, but in Quincy, which was a sizeable town.

8 Divide the class into imaginary family teams and instruct them to decide as a family what must be done to relocate to a new home. They should consider these questions:

1) Why do you want to move to the wilderness?
2) What supplies will be absolutely necessary?
3) What provisions must be made for those left behind?
4) What kind of farm do you want to establish?
5) Will it be one for profit or just self-sufficiency?
6) When is the best time to leave?
7) Should you all go at once or in groups?

Have students write a dramatization of their imaginary family's discussions and present it to the class. They may use costumes, make scenery or use props. When rehearsals are finished, invite parents to come and see the dramatizations.

9 As an evaluation tool, ask students to make a list of "suspense" words—words they would use to create a feeling of suspense in a story. (*Examples: mysterious, shadows, stealthily, etc.*)

LESSON 3 (CHAPTERS 5-7)

1 Continue with selected vocabulary studies. Ask a student to look up the word "intimidate" in a dictionary and read the definition to the class *(to make another feel awkward, inferior or shy)*. Allow volunteers to tell about situations when they might have felt intimidated by another. Ask a different student to look up the definition of "grace" and read it aloud *(undeserved free favor from God)*. Give students time to read verses in God's Word about His grace. Have a class discussion about what these verses tell us about God's love for us. *(In His eyes we are His creation and He designed us to be exactly as He wants. To know God designed each person in His image with abilities He chose frees us from allowing ourselves to be intimidated by another.)* Suggested verses are: Romans 3:24; Romans 6:14; 2 Timothy 2:1; Titus 3:7; Genesis 1:31; Psalm 84:11. Students may also look in their concordances under the word "good."

2 Read Chapters 5–7. Ask students to point out a passage that verifies Matt's feelings of intimidation by the expressionless Attean. *(The passage is in Chapter 6. The paragraph points out that Matt felt like a fool because of his injured leg and Attean's defiant attitude.)*

3 Read Chapter 5 again, paying attention to Matt's reaction when he realized, even in his badly injured state, that it was an Indian man standing over him reaching out for his throat. Questions for discussion:

1) Why would Matt try to jerk away from someone who has just rescued him? *(experiences in recent years of wars between Indians and English colonists)*

2) Review Chapters 6–7. Note Attean's anger and defiance toward Matt. Why would he have these feelings for someone he does not know? *(same reason)*

3) Ask students to look up Ephesians 4:32 in their Bible. *("Be kind and compassionate to one another, forgiving each other, just as in Christ God forgave you" [NIV].)* How would application of this verse help Matt and Attean forget past hurts and reach out to one another with compassion and understanding? *(Their hearts would be softened toward each other and they would not be feeling so "I" oriented.)*

4 Saknis is from the family of the beaver. Use **Master 3.1** to have students

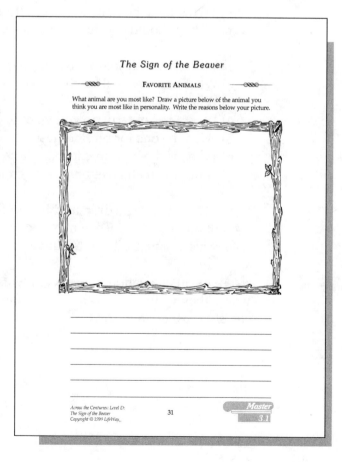

Across the Centuries: Level D
The Sign of the Beaver

choose an animal to compare to their own personalities. Reading a book like *The Treasure Tree* by Trent and Smalley will help students understand what is meant by comparing personality traits.

5 Focus on the author's description of the honeybees. After studying the honeybee, it is impossible to think that such an insect, so suited physically and instinctively to perform its tasks for survival, just came into being by mere chance. The clear imprint of the Designer is apparent when more is learned about the bee's behavior. God's creation is a powerful witness to His existence. Distribute copies of **Master 3.2a** and **b,** copied back to back, and instruct students to read and follow the directions.

6 Ask students what two books they would take into the wilderness with them if they had been in Matt's position. Pass out two sheets of drawing paper and tell students to design book covers for the two books they would choose. Covers should include book title, author and an interesting illustration of the story or characters. If the Bible is one of their choices, allow them to be creative in designing its cover.

7 Invite the school nurse or a doctor to come to the class and discuss how to assist a person who has been stung by bees or bitten by some other poisonous insect or animal. Discuss the dangers of bee stings if the person is allergic to its venom.

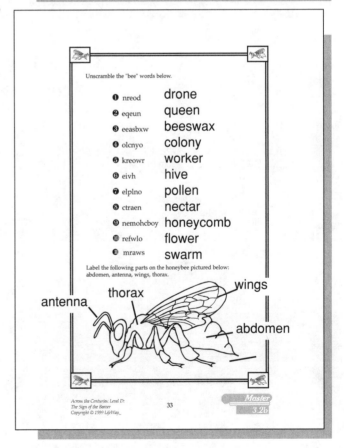

8 Why was Saknis so determined for Attean to learn to read the books and words written by the white man? *(The white men had made peace with the Indians by writing treaties that the Indians could not read. The Indians put their mark on the treaties as a sign of friendship. They had no idea they were signing away their homelands. Saknis wanted Attean to be able to prevent that from happening in the future.)*

9 As a culminating activity for Lesson 3, pass out copies of **Master 3.3**. Go over the Indian signs together. Allow the class to find others to put on a chart or to write on the board. Give each student a large grocery bag. Have them cut off the least printed side and wad it up. When it is opened again it should resemble a piece of animal hide. They may trim it into the shape of a bear or buffalo hide if they desire. Instruct the students to write a message to a classmate using the Indian symbols discussed. Tell them to make it colorful, as Indians often used dyes to write their picture messages and records. Display the "hides" on the bulletin board or in the hall.

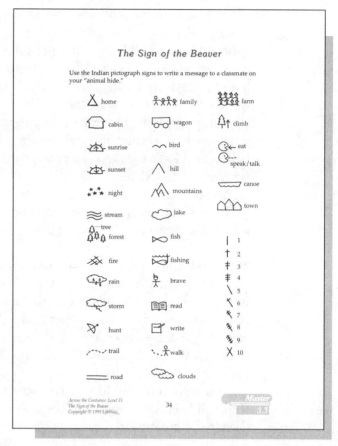

LESSON 4 (CHAPTERS 8-10)

1 Give students time to make and review flash cards for the vocabulary words in Lessons 1–4. As an alternative activity, divide the class into two teams. Hold up a flash card for each student in turn to give the definition. Conduct the game like a spelling bee. Reward the final two students with bookmarks or extra library time.

2 Read Chapters 8–10 and discuss the major events.

1) How did Matt's opinion of Robinson Crusoe change at the end of Chapter 8? (*Attean pointed out that Crusoe needed all the tools he salvaged from the shipwreck to build his shelter on the island. The Indian, according to Attean, needs none of that to survive. He is much smarter than the white man. Matt realized what he and his father had accomplished with one axe and an adz when they arrived in the wilderness, and Crusoe no longer seemed to be the hero he was before.*)

2) Ask a student to read the passage from *Robinson Crusoe* in Chapter 9. Why did this passage anger Attean so much that he left the cabin? (*A native of any kind bowing as a slave to a white man greatly offended Attean. He would rather die.*)

3) What seemed like a natural situation to Matt now troubles him. How was his thinking beginning to change about white men being superior to others? (*He saw Attean's reaction and maybe for the first time understood that no man is superior to another. Explain to students that this was a turning point in the story for Matt. From this point, he longed to impress Attean as he recognized the young brave's superiority in survival skills.*)

3 Ask students to locate Scriptures that indicate that in the eyes of Jesus we are all the same. (*Acts 10:34–35; Ephesians 2:19–22; Romans 2:11; 10:12.*) If we are Christians, we are brothers and sisters in Christ. What does that mean? Should this fact change the way that we treat people?

4 Instruct students to design a snare or trap to catch an animal. Ask them to draw their design on **Master 4.1**. Tell them to make the trap that will not injure the animal. Discuss reasons why that is the best kind of trap to use.

Across the Centuries: Level D
The Sign of the Beaver

5 A snare is a trap disguised to trick an animal by enticing it with something tempting to eat. As Christians, we also have a tempter who sets "snares" for us to trap us into committing what we know to be sin. This tempter does not show himself to be evil or frightening. That would tip us off right away! Rather, he disguises himself—sometimes as an angel of light. This tempter was waiting for Eve in the Garden of Eden (Genesis 3:1–7). This tempter is, of course, Satan. Let students look up the following verses: 1 Peter 5:8; John 8:44; 2 Corinthians 11:14. These verses tell us that Satan spends his time setting "snares" for God's people. He is interested in Christians because God is his enemy, and Satan's goal is to prevent God's work from being done. Distribute **Master 4.2** and ask students to circle words on the page that are examples of Satan's "snares."

1 Peter 5:8 (NIV): *Be self-controlled and alert. Your enemy the devil prowls around like a roaring lion looking for someone to devour.*

John 8:44 (NIV): *He (the devil) was a murderer from the beginning, not holding to the truth, for there is no truth in him. When he lies, he speaks his native language, for he is a liar and the father of lies.*

2 Corinthians 11:14 (NIV): *And no wonder, for Satan himself masquerades as an angel of light.*

6 Divide the class into groups. Allow each group to decide on a national park or forest they would like to research. Remind the students to include activities, scenery, location, sight-seeing tours, and anything else that would draw vacationers. They can find out if there are any Indian reservations near the park and research the customs of the local Native Americans. If possible, allow the students to do some of their research on the Internet. After the research is complete, each group should produce a travel poster and a brochure. They can include the importance of safety rules in their brochures as to first aid, leaving food exposed, campfires and how to be sure they are safely extinguished, use of matches and availability of emergency services. Give each group time to present its poster and brochure to the class.

7 Choose other adventure books and stories for a classroom library. Allow students to go in pairs to younger classes to read some of the stories.

8 To evaluate Lesson 4, ask students to write a brief paragraph stating the main idea of each chapter read in Lesson 4. Allow them to re-read Chapters 8–10 if necessary. The paragraph should bring out the point that Matt began to think that the white man is perhaps not always superior to everyone else. He demonstrated his doubts as he tried hard to compete with Attean and impress him with his skills of survival, only to be humiliated in defeat with each attempt.

Lesson 5 (Chapters 11-14)

1 Continue with vocabulary introduction and study. Assign the reading of Chapters 11–14 and generally discuss the main ideas.

2 Especially discuss some of the secret signs Attean left along the forest trail *(beaver sign, broken twigs, stones stacked a specific way, tufts of grass hanging from trees or bushes)*.

3 Distribute **Master 5.1**. Instruct students to mark the wilderness trail by adding signs along the path they want to take to the river. On the back, they can write directions to someone seeking the way to the river. In the directions, instruct them to use rebus pictographs that match the signs used to mark the trail.

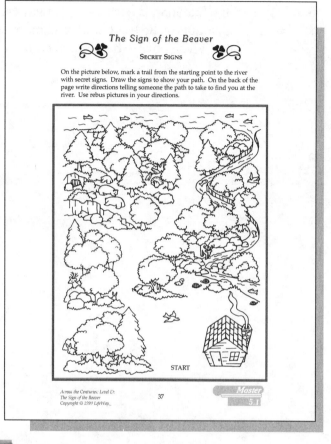

4 Instruct students to compare and contrast the story of Noah (Genesis 7, 8 and 9) and the story of Gluskabe using **Master 5.2**.

The Sign of the Beaver

Noah and Gluskabe

On the Venn diagram below compare and contrast Matt's story of Noah from the Bible and Attean's story of Gluskabe handed down by his people.

Gluskabe: Before animals climbed the high hill and then tree, he sent ducks. Mud in duck's mouth. Gluskabe made grass, birds, beaver, all other Indians. Story began with man.

Both: Flood. Noah safe in ark; Indian safe on high hill in high tree. Used birds to see if waters had dried.

Noah: God warned Noah. Noah built an ark, took his family inside, sent a dove that returned with an olive branch. The story began with God.

Across the Centuries: Level D
The Sign of the Beaver
Copyright © 1999 LifeWay™

5 Distribute copies of **Master 5.3**. Instruct students to match the Indian signs to the words they symbolize. Allow sufficient time for all to finish and discuss the choices they made. Assign some students the task of drawing the hand signs on a large chart and allow a different student to write the matching words. As students finish daily work, allow them to find more Indian sign language and add what they find to the chart. This chart represents hand signs. Discuss how they are different from pictographs.

6 To evaluate Lesson 5, ask students to write an opinion paragraph about Attean. Write these questions on the board:

1) What do you admire about him?
2) What do you find frustrating about him?
3) What are his strengths and weaknesses?
4) Why do you have the right to judge his behavior?

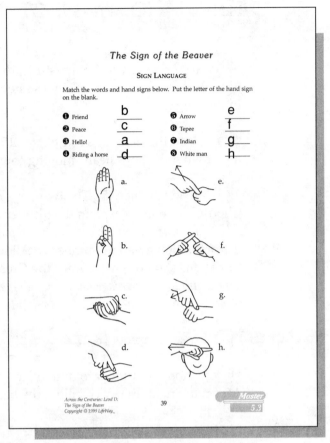

LESSON 6 (CHAPTERS 15-17)

1 To continue vocabulary study, discuss and provide models, then instruct each student to write an original sentence with each of the new vocabulary words in Lesson 6.

2 Read the first page of Chapter 15. Choose a student to make a prediction about what the boys heard moving toward them through the woods.

3 Read Chapter 15. The two boys reacted differently to the killing of the bear. Choose students to explain the difference. (*Matt laughed to hide his trembling; Attean asked forgiveness from the bear for being forced to kill her.*) Dramatize the scene. Verify the prediction given in number 2. Allow students to discuss the attitudes Christians should have toward the Creation. (*Genesis 1:28 commands mankind to have dominion, or management, over all creation. This should be done with care and respect. However, we are not to worship things that were created [Romans 1:18–25].*)

4 Read Chapters 16–17.

5 Choose a student to dramatize Attean telling the story of killing the bear.

6 Re-read the description of the Indian village as Matt saw it in the daylight. Divide the class into two groups. Assign one group the task of drawing a mural of the Indian village on a long sheet of paper. Allow them to use their books to assure all the details given are included in the mural. Instruct the second group to draw a mural depicting Matt's log home showing the cleared land, the corn fields, garden and trails leading out to the forest wilderness. Allow them to search the story for details given about Matt's home. Display the murals in the hall when complete.

7 Assign **Master 6.1** to evaluate information learned from Chapters 15–17.

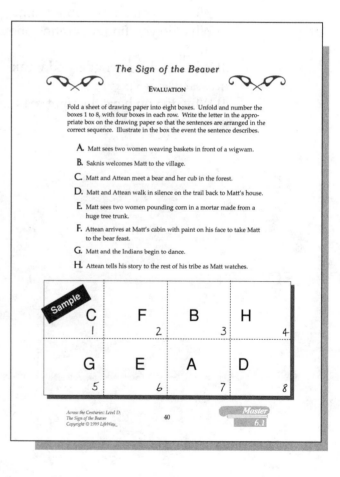

Across the Centuries: Level D
The Sign of the Beaver

LESSON 7 (CHAPTERS 18-22)

1. Discuss the new vocabulary for Lesson 7. Have students illustrate the definitions on the board.

2. Present the class with a vocabulary challenge. With the words from all the lessons visible, read the definitions of ten words and instruct students to write each word. Next, read ten words and instruct students to write the correct definitions in their own words. Choose an appropriate reward for those who achieve a previously specified percentage of correct answers. Rewards might include homework passes, library passes, lunch with the teacher or free time passes.

3. Read Chapter 18. Discuss Matt's increasing concern about the length of time his father has been gone. If Matt has accumulated ten sticks with seven notches on each stick, how many days has his father been gone? *(70)*

4. On chart paper write a list of possible reasons Matt's family was so late coming home. Keep the chart displayed and verify the reason when it is discovered.

5. If possible, find an animal trap (or picture) similar to the steel one that trapped Attean's dog. Allow the students to examine it and discuss their thoughts on the use of such a trap.

6. Read Chapters 19–22.

7. Allow students to research the game of lacrosse (also called field hockey). With modifications, for safety reasons, allow the class to play a game of lacrosse. Decide what can be used safely for lacrosse sticks and discuss ahead of time appropriate boundaries and safety procedures. Supervise the game closely. Ask another adult to assist with the game.

8. Distribute **Master 7.1**. Lead a brief discussion pointing out the differences between the boys' views of the land, based on their individual cultures. *(Attean: land is free to all, cannot belong to anyone, compared it to air we breathe. Matt: land can be bought and sold, fought for, taken from those unable to keep it.)* Review directions together for **Master 7.1**.

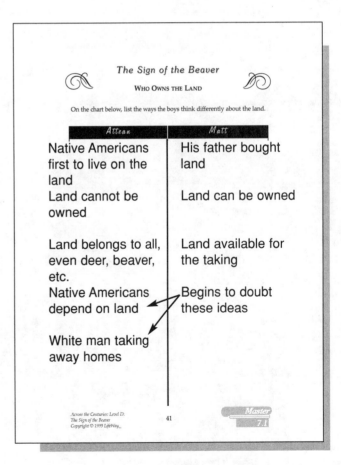

9 If Matt had time to keep a journal, he surely would have written about ways his opinions have changed regarding Native Americans, especially Attean. Distribute copies of **Master 7.2**. Instruct students to write a journal page from Matt's point of view. Begin the page with the following sentence: *I am not so sure now who owns this land.* Have the students fold the master into a mini book.

10 Use **Master 7.3** as an evaluation of cumulative information through Lesson 7.

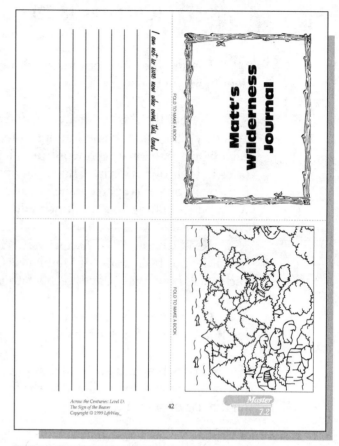

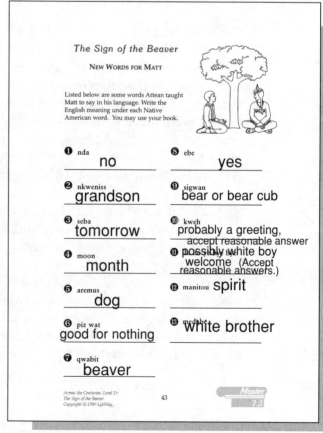

LESSON 8 (CHAPTERS 23-25)

1 Complete a vocabulary study and assign the reading of Chapters 23–25.

2 Discuss the reason Matt's family has taken so long to arrive *(typhus)*. Compare the reason to the predictions made previously.

3 Matt and Attean have both reached manhood and earned the approval of the authorities in their lives. What is similar about their accomplishments? *(Both survived being alone in the wilderness.)* Allow students to expand on this idea through class discussion.

4 Matt and Attean learned from each other in spite of their differences. Distribute copies of **Master 8.1** for students to compare what each boy learned.

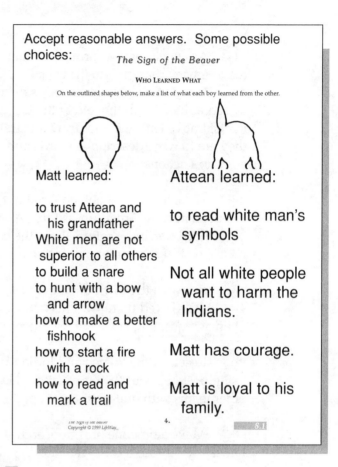

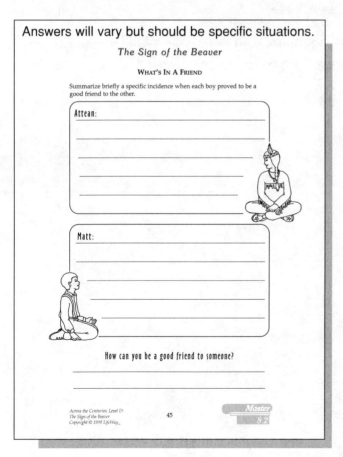

5 Discuss qualities the students expect in their true friends: trust, concern, loyalty, respect, etc. Distribute copies of **Master 8.2** and review directions with students.

ENRICHMENT

1 As an alternative form of evaluation, let students make a flip chart of each of the following characters in the book: Matt, Saknis, Attean, Ben, Good-for-nothing-dog. Provide five large index cards or construction paper to each student to be folded in half. With the fold at the top, they are to write the name of the character in decorative lettering and draw illustrations on the cover. On the inside page, they are to write descriptive words and phrases of the character's personality, character and actions.

2 Make individual notebooks about different Native American tribes and their locations in early American history. Assign each student a specific tribe. Include in the notebook information about the customs, homes, food, and beliefs specific to the tribe. Pictures, drawings and maps should be included in the notebook.

3 Research the town of Quincy, Massachusetts, during the period that Matt would have lived there with his family. Write to the Chamber of Commerce in Quincy requesting any available historical information.

4 Research the French and Indian War. Have student teams present reports using posters about the information they discover. Each team can challenge the other teams with questions developed from the report.

5 Make a timeline of American history beginning with the settlement of Jamestown through the Westward Expansion, ending just prior to the Civil War.

The Sign of the Beaver

CHANGING VERBS TO NOUNS USING R, ER AND OR

Change each of the following verbs into nouns by adding the appropriate suffix: *r, er, or*. Write a definition of the noun in your own words. Use the noun in an original sentence. Use the following example as a pattern.

Example: *dance* + *er* is *dancer*; someone who dances
Sentence: The ballet dancer leaped gracefully into the air.

❶ teach _____

❷ hunt _____

❸ erase _____

❹ farm _____

❺ explore _____

❻ travel _____

❼ trespass _____

❽ command _____

❾ preach _____

❿ survey _____

Across the Centuries: Level D:
The Sign of the Beaver
Copyright © 1999 LifeWay™

The Sign of the Beaver

 A Note of Encouragement

Write a letter to Matt telling him of God's promises in Psalm 23.

Dear Matt,

_____

_____

_____

_____

_____

_____

_____

_____

_____

_____

_____

Your friend,

_____

The Sign of the Beaver

 ## A Colonial Recipe

Decorate around the following recipe for hasty pudding. Cut it out and glue it to a large card. Add details to make it look like a recipe card.

Hasty Pudding

Put some water and salt in a heavy saucepan and bring it to the boil. Pour in some yellow cornmeal very slowly. Stir constantly until mixture is thick enough for a spoon to stand up in it. Dip the pudding into 4 small bowls, put a dab of butter on top of each serving, sprinkle with ground nutmeg and pour on some molasses. Serve hot.

The Sign of the Beaver

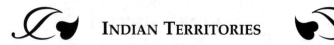

INDIAN TERRITORIES

Locate the areas on the colonial map below where each of the following Native American tribes lived: Iroquois, Penobscot, Mohegan, Delaware, Susquehanna, Mohawk, Powhatan.

Challenge! Locate the homes of other tribes and write their names.

Across the Centuries: Level D:
The Sign of the Beaver
Copyright © 1999 LifeWay™

The Sign of the Beaver

FAVORITE ANIMALS

What animal are you most like? Draw a picture below of the animal you think you are most like in personality. Write the reasons below your picture.

_____

_____

_____

_____

_____

_____

The Sign of the Beaver

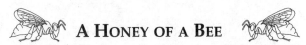 **A Honey of a Bee**

Honeybees depend on the nectar in flowers to supply them with food and ingredients needed to make honey. Flowers depend on honeybees to take pollen from flower to flower so new flowers can grow. Every part of a honebee's body serves a specific function for the bee to survive and produce more bees. Each bee knows the job it must do to sustain the life of the colony. Are bees the only creatures with this instinctive nature? Take the time to observe Creation. How do spiders know when to spin their webs? Why does the ocean stay within its confined space? How do the leaves know when it is time to fall from the trees? How do the trees know when it is time to bud out? Why do you get thirsty? Why does your heart beat continually even when you sleep? Read the following verses in your Bible so that you will be certain of the answers: Psalm 89:9, 11-12; Psalm 95:4-5; Psalm 96:11-12; Psalm 104.

Read about honeybees in an encyclopedia or other books on insects. Answer the following questions.

❶ How many sides does each cell in a honeycomb have? _____

❷ What three kinds of bees occupy a bee hive?
_____   _____   _____

❸ How does the bee carry flower nectar back to the hive?
_____
_____

❹ Explain how the beehive is made.
_____
_____

❺ How do the bees use the cells in the beehive?
_____
_____

❻ Explain how the worker bee tells the other bees where food is to be found.
_____
_____

Across the Centuries: Level D:
The Sign of the Beaver
Copyright © 1999 LifeWay™

Master 3.2a

Unscramble the "bee" words below.

① nreod _____

② eqeun _____

③ eeasbxw _____

④ olcnyo _____

⑤ kreowr _____

⑥ eivh _____

⑦ elplno _____

⑧ ctraen _____

⑨ nemohcboy _____

⑩ refwlo _____

⑪ mraws _____

Label the following parts on the honeybee pictured below: abdomen, antenna, wings, thorax.

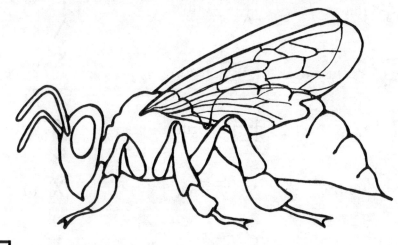

Across the Centuries: Level D:
The Sign of the Beaver
Copyright © 1999 LifeWay™

The Sign of the Beaver

Use the Indian pictograph signs to write a message to a classmate on your "animal hide."

home   family   farm

cabin   wagon   climb

sunrise   bird   eat

sunset   hill   speak/talk

night   mountains   canoe

stream   lake   town

tree
forest   fish   1

fire   fishing   2

                        3

rain   brave   4

                        5

storm   read   6

                        7

hunt   write   8

                        9

trail   walk   10

road   clouds

Across the Centuries: Level D:
The Sign of the Beaver
Copyright © 1999 LifeWay™

The Sign of the Beaver

Design a snare that will entrap the rabbit on this page so you can have rabbit stew for an evening meal.

The Sign of the Beaver

 WATCH OUT FOR SNARES

Circle the words below that might catch you in a "snare."

argue

gossip

pray

steal

obey

forget to obey

pout

LIE

SERVE

grumble

humble

pride

ignore people

kindness

work hard

give

cheat

forgiveness

encourage

feel pitiful

The Sign of the Beaver

Secret Signs

On the picture below, mark a trail from the starting point to the river with secret signs. Draw the signs to show your path. On the back of the page write directions telling someone the path to take to find you at the river. Use rebus pictures in your directions.

START

The Sign of the Beaver

Noah and Gluskabe

On the Venn diagram below compare and contrast Matt's story of Noah from the Bible and Attean's story of Gluskabe handed down by his people.

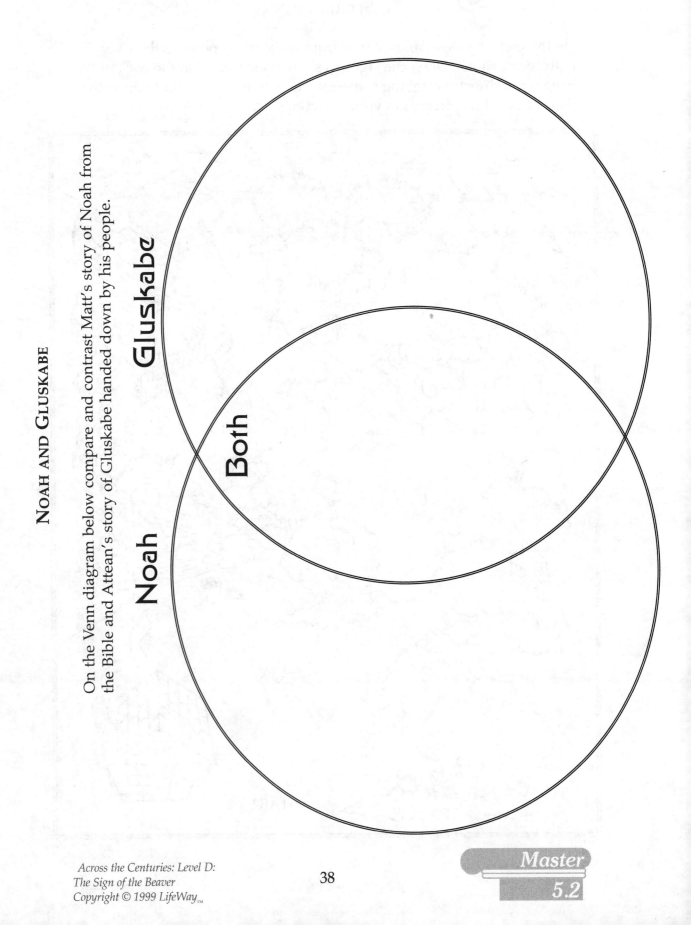

Across the Centuries: Level D:
The Sign of the Beaver
Copyright © 1999 LifeWay

Master 5.2

The Sign of the Beaver

SIGN LANGUAGE

Match the words and hand signs below. Put the letter of the hand sign on the blank.

❶ Friend _____   ❺ Arrow _____

❷ Peace _____   ❻ Tepee _____

❸ Hello! _____   ❼ Indian _____

❹ Riding a horse _____   ❽ White man _____

 a.

 e.

 b.

 f.

 c.

 g.

 h.

The Sign of the Beaver

EVALUATION

Fold a sheet of drawing paper into eight boxes. Unfold and number the boxes 1 to 8, with four boxes in each row. Write the letter in the appropriate box on the drawing paper so that the sentences are arranged in the correct sequence. Illustrate in the box the event the sentence describes.

A. Matt sees two women weaving baskets in front of a wigwam.

B. Saknis welcomes Matt to the village.

C. Matt and Attean meet a bear and her cub in the forest.

D. Matt and Attean walk in silence on the trail back to Matt's house.

E. Matt sees two women pounding corn in a mortar made from a huge tree trunk.

F. Attean arrives at Matt's cabin with paint on his face to take Matt to the bear feast.

G. Matt and the Indians begin to dance.

H. Attean tells his story to the rest of his tribe as Matt watches.

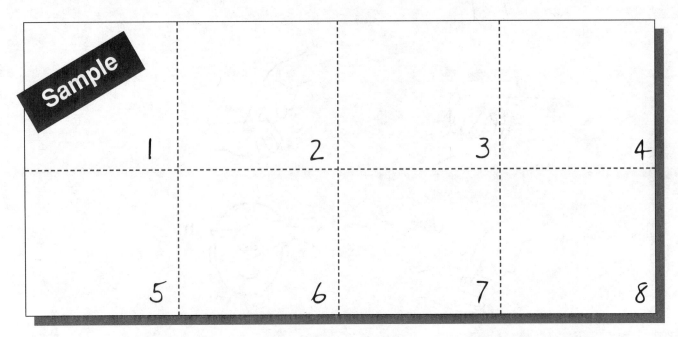

Across the Centuries: Level D:
The Sign of the Beaver
Copyright © 1999 LifeWay™

40

Master 6.1

The Sign of the Beaver

WHO OWNS THE LAND

On the chart below, list the ways the boys think differently about the land.

Attean	Matt

I am not so sure now who owns this land.

FOLD TO MAKE A BOOK

FOLD TO MAKE A BOOK

Across the Centuries: Level D:
The Sign of the Beaver
Copyright © 1999 LifeWay™

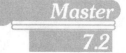

The Sign of the Beaver

NEW WORDS FOR MATT

Listed below are some words Attean taught Matt to say in his language. Write the English meaning under each Native American word. You may use your book.

❶ nda

_____

❷ nkweniss

_____

❸ seba

_____

❹ moon

_____

❺ aremus

_____

❻ piz wat

_____

❼ qwabit

_____

❽ ebe

_____

❾ sigwan

_____

❿ kweh

_____

⓫ Ta ho ye bye bye

_____

⓬ manitou

_____

⓭ medabe

_____

Across the Centuries: Level D:
The Sign of the Beaver
Copyright © 1999 LifeWay

The Sign of the Beaver

WHO LEARNED WHAT

On the outlined shapes below, make a list of what each boy learned from the other.

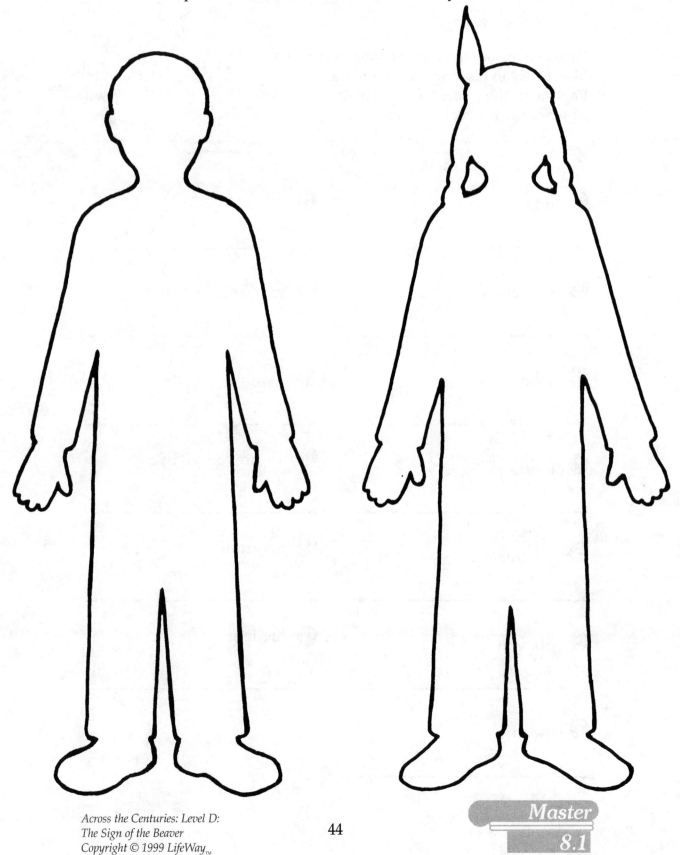

*Across the Centuries: Level D:
The Sign of the Beaver
Copyright © 1999 LifeWay*™

The Sign of the Beaver

What's In A Friend

Summarize briefly a specific incidence when each boy proved to be a good friend to the other.

Attean:
_____
_____
_____
_____
_____

Matt:
_____
_____
_____
_____
_____

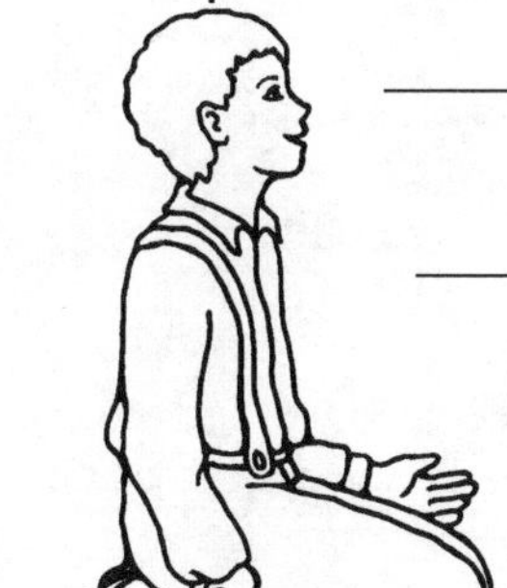

How can you be a good friend to someone?
_____
_____

From the Mixed-Up Files of Mrs. Basil E. Frankweiler

by E. L. Konigsburg

This Newbery Award winner mixes adventure, mystery and a touch of fantasy in a totally improbable setting. The children in the story realize that sometimes the planning of an adventure is even more satisfying than the adventure itself, except when you experience a change. In this sense the book reflects the Christian life—being reborn and becoming involved in a new adventure that changes believers in ever new and exciting ways.

OBJECTIVES:

1 Students will effectively use a range of strategies to decode and understand the meaning of new vocabulary.

2 Students will summarize the main idea and relevant details of the text.

3 Students will describe and sequence the major events in the text.

4 Students will use research skills to prepare reports on collateral subjects.

5 Students will present their research findings using different media such as written and oral reports, posters, games, audio and video presentations.

6 Students will analyze and describe how the character qualities of Claudia and Jamie enabled them to successfully achieve their adventure.

7 Students will cite examples of the teamwork displayed by Claudia and Jamie and will use team strategies in various activities.

8 Students will identify the plot twist the author develops to add a new dimension to the story.

9 Students will use math skills to project money needs and prepare a budget.

10 Students will use map-reading skills to locate places mentioned in the text.

11 Students will find examples in Scripture where preparation, planning and perseverance led to success.

12 Students will recognize that an inner change results from spiritual growth, which determines the character and integrity of an individual.

SUMMARY OF THE STORY:

Claudia Kincaid decided that, as the oldest child and only girl in her family, she was vastly under-appreciated. As a way to teach the rest of the family a lesson, she decided to run away. She wanted to be sure that her home away from home was one of comfort and beauty, so she decided on the Metropolitan Museum of Art as her destination. Her younger brother Jamie became her partner in this adventure because of character qualities he possessed. Their preparation and perseverance made them successful not only in the planned adventure, but also in solving a mystery. In the end, the children learned that a change within yourself is the most satisfactory accomplishment of all.

ABOUT THE AUTHOR:

E. L. Konigsburg was born in New York but grew up in Pennsylvania. She majored in chemistry in college and worked as a chemist, doing research and teaching after graduation. She didn't start her writing career until after she was married and had three children. Most of her books were named American Library Association Notable Children's Books. In addition to being an excellent author, Mrs. Konigsburg is a gifted artist and has illustrated a number of books. *From the Mixed-Up Files of Mrs. Basil E. Frankweiler* won the Newbery Medal and *Jennifer, Hecate, Macbeth, William McKinley, and Me, Elizabeth* was named a Newbery Honor Book. Mrs. Konigsburg lives with her family near Jacksonville, Florida, and enjoys drawing, painting, reading and walking along the beach.

INSTRUCTIONAL PLAN

PREPARATION FOR READING:

1 Collect books and pictures of the Italian Renaissance, especially the works of Michelangelo and Leonardo da Vinci. If possible have replicas of some of Michelangelo's statues.

2 Since the major portion of this story takes place in and around the Metropolitan Museum of Art in New York City, have students share their experiences in visiting museums. Make a list of different kinds of museums: art, science, history, transportation, folklore or folk/country music museums. Assign teams of students to research the kinds of exhibits found in each. Students can use copies of **Master P.1** to chart the findings. After sharing research findings, students may design a museum mural or design a collage of the different type of museums and the exhibits they contain.

3 Compare the differences between living in a large city (New York) and living in a small town. Obtain and display pictures and maps of New York City. Tour brochures make interesting reading and often include maps of the area around major attractions. Travel videos and the Travel Channel (cable TV) are usually available to highlight city experiences. After students review this material, allow them to work on copies of **Master P.2**. On the left side, students can list things that will be found only in the large city. On the right side they can list those things found only in a small town. In the middle, those things common to both can be listed.

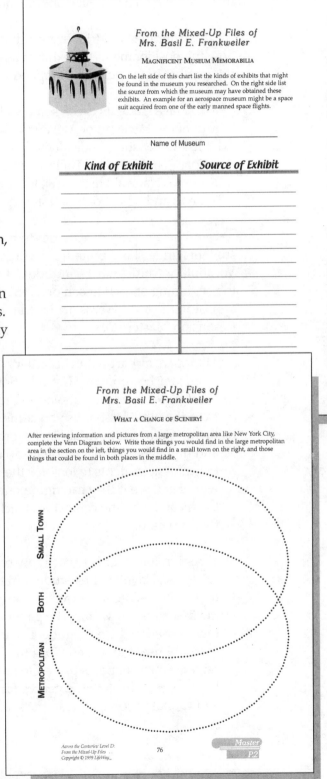

4 Invite the art teacher or a local artist/sculptor to share experiences with the class. Invite the speaker to explain the steps involved in the creation of a piece of art from the idea through the culmination of the work.

5 Plan a field trip to a museum in your area. Discuss the kinds of exhibits that will be seen and assign specific questions regarding the exhibits.

6 After the field trip, draw a diagram of the layout of the museum. Discuss how the positioning of the exhibits affected the way the exhibits were viewed and the number of viewers who stopped to see them.

7 Have students check some Web sites of major museums, (e.g., the Metropolitan Museum of Art) and download pictures of some of the current exhibits. Other suggestions include the American History, Natural History, Air/Space, and National Gallery of the Smithsonian Institution; the Chicago Museum of Natural History (Field Museum); Museum of Science and Industry (Chicago); and others of local interest.

8 Use a variety of activities to help students understand unfamiliar words. Vocabulary words may be introduced at the beginning of each lesson or as they appear in the text. Words are listed by lessons on **Master P.3**.

1) Prepare a chart with vocabulary words for Lesson One. Use additional chart paper to add vocabulary words from the other lessons as you come to them. Go over the vocabulary words and highlight the ones students do not know. Ask students to look for the words and see if they can figure out the meaning by the context in which they are used.

2) Assign four words to each row of students. Have the first student in the row write a sentence correctly using the first assigned word. The paper is then passed to the next student who correctly uses the second word in a sentence. The paper is passed to succeeding students in the same manner. The last students check the sentences for correctness of usage, spelling, punctuation and capitalization then read the sentences to the class.

From the Mixed-Up Files of Mrs. Basil E. Frankweiler

VOCABULARY

Lesson One - Chapters 1 and 2
injustice
monotony
mah-jong
ventured
elegant
Manhattan
fiscal week
Neanderthal man
mutual
tycoon
boodle
percolator
commuters

Lesson Two - Chapter 3
extravagant
cheapskate
inconspicuous
matinee
Chancellor of the Exchequer
Marie Antoinette
ornately
alleged
fussbudget
English Renaissance
orthopedic shoes

Lesson Three - Chapter 4
automat
perilous
Italian Renaissance
impostors
embalm
acquisitions
Michelangelo
Prince Franz Josef II
curator
Bologna
hodgepodge
mediocre

Lesson Four - Chapter 5
laundromat
pagan
corpuscle
Mona Lisa
petit fours
espresso

Lesson Five - Chapters 6 and 7
stealthily
browsing
Congressional Medal of Honor

Rockefeller Center
Sistine Chapel
Mohammed
quarterly
drizzle
mastaba
familiarity

Lesson Six - Chapter 8
abrasions
sari
consensus
derby hat
counterfeited

Lesson Seven - Chapter 9
paupers
baroque
spigot
commotion
sauntered

Lesson Eight - Chapter 10
preoccupied
maimed
deceased
bequeathing

3) Direct students to use a thesaurus to find synonyms or antonyms for words. They can build a glossary of vocabulary words.

4) Let students design a crossword puzzle or word search using ten of the vocabulary words. They can use the meanings as clues. Be sure they prepare an answer key on another sheet.

5) Assign each student a word to illustrate on a 3" x 5" card. They can write the word on the front of the card. Use student illustrations as flash cards.

6) Divide the class into teams and play "Hangman" with the words.

7) Allow students to prepare quizzes to give to each other. Be sure they place answers on another sheet of paper.

LESSON 1 (CHAPTERS 1 AND 2)

1 Read the introduction with the students. Explain that this story is Mrs. Basil E. Frankweiler's account of this adventure. Instruct students to be looking for examples that indicate this throughout the story. Ask students why they think Mrs. Frankweiler is writing this to her lawyer. What might this tell them about what to expect in the book?

2 Assign a discussion group to address each of the following questions. Distribute the questions on slips of paper. Set up posters around the room. Ask the groups to list their answers to the questions on the posters then present the information to the class.

1) What would be a parent's reaction to a child running away?
2) What are the reasons why teenagers run away?
3) What are the reasons why children run away?
4) What should parents do the moment they hear their child wants to run away?
5) What are the signs of a potential runaway?
6) What should brothers or sisters do if they know a sibling is going to run away?

3 Direct class discussion of the following:

1) Why was Claudia's plan to run away the wrong thing to do?

2) What are the dangers to children or teens who run away?

3) How does running away violate the fifth commandment, "Honor your father and your mother" (Exodus 20:12), and the admonition to obedience in Ephesians 6:1?

4) What other ways can you suggest to help Claudia get the appreciation she thinks she deserves?

4 List various ways of showing appreciation on the board or on chart paper. Distribute copies of **Master 1.1** and allow students to design appreciation notes to those they want to acknowledge.

5 Assign the reading of the rest of Chapter 1.

6 After completing the chapter, ask students if they believe Claudia's plan will be successful and to explain why or why not. Elicit the response that careful planning is essential to a successful outcome. Ask why Jamie was a good choice as a companion.

7 Distribute copies of **Master 1.2** for students to complete. Compare students' lists with Claudia's preparations in Chapter 1.

8 Distribute copies of **Master 1.3** to pairs of students. After the teams have worked for several minutes, assign them to draw large backpacks on chart paper and fill them with things that are absolutely necessary. They can color the backpacks, cut them out and hang them from the ceiling.

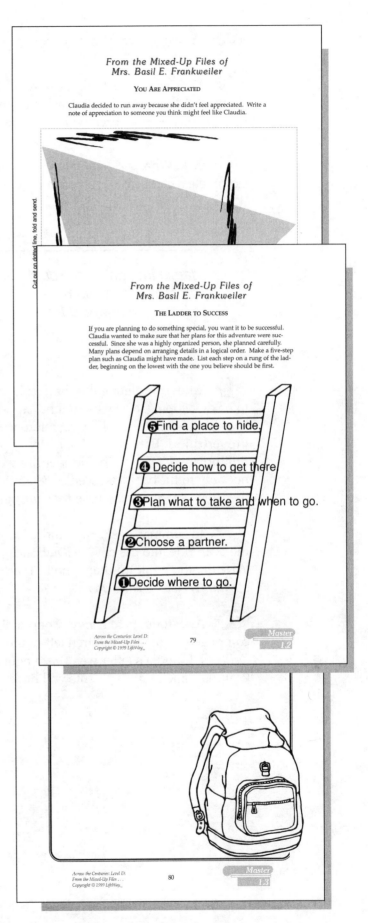

9 Assign the reading of Chapter 2.

10 Direct students to find examples of Claudia's careful planning in this chapter. As these are located, ask students to write them in their literature journals, predicting how each will affect the plan.

11 Ask: What did Jamie think was happening? What were Claudia's ideas? Complete a chart from information given.

Jamie's Ideas	Claudia's Ideas
Jamie thought they would be camping out somewhere. They would be "roughing it."	They would go to the Metropolitan Museum of Art. They would be living in luxury.

12 After completing the chart, ask students to list other conflicts that appeared to be developing, and what might happen if they cannot be resolved. Direct them to look up one of the following references that relate to conflict resolution: Proverbs 15:1; Ephesians 4:26; James 1:19; Proverbs 21:23; Romans 14:19; Philippians 2:3. They should identify ways in which these verses can be applied not only to the conflicts faced by Claudia and Jamie, but also to conflicts they themselves face. Allow time for sharing.

13 In summary, ask: How did Claudia's and Jamie's attitudes change during the train ride into the city? *(Claudia delegated authority over the money to Jamie.)* Why do you think this happened? *(Each now had a reason to make the adventure successful. They were partners.)*

14 Ask students to review Chapter 2 to find out what other task had to be completed before the children left home. *(A goodbye note to their parents had to be written.)* Claudia's letter was very vague. Have students discuss the response Claudia's and Jamie's parents will have. What response would your parents have?

Across the Centuries: Level D:
From the Mixed-Up Files...

Lesson 2 (Chapter 3)

1 Vocabulary words may be introduced now as a group, or may be discussed as they are encountered in the chapter.

2 Have a map of the greater New York City area available. Be sure the map includes the border city of Greenwich, Connecticut. Locate Greenwich on the map and trace the route into New York City, ending at Grand Central Station.

3 Ask students to draw their own New York City maps with illustrations of the most famous tourist spots.

4 Read and discuss the first two pages of the chapter. Be sure students take note of the change in roles displayed by Claudia and Jamie. Point out that each block is approximately one-tenth of a mile. Ask students to calculate the number of miles the children must walk to reach their destination. You may want to have the students trace the route on a map of this area.

5 As you continue reading this chapter, ask students to explain why Claudia was experiencing a growing sense of frustration during the walk and how Jamie's remark about her brilliance diffused the situation. Which principle of conflict resolution did Jamie use? *(Romans 14:19: follow peace, edify one another)* This discussion should lead into **Master 2.1**. In this activity, students can analyze the character traits exhibited by Claudia and Jamie. Ask students to look for specific situations in this chapter and then to list them on the master. Plan to continue this activity throughout the rest of the text.

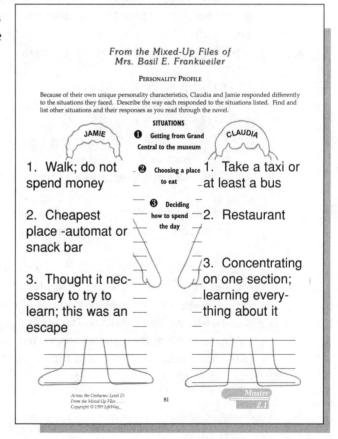

Across the Centuries: Level D:
From the Mixed-Up Files . . .

6 Distribute **Master 2.2**, Map of the Museum, for students to locate the various places mentioned and to follow the routes taken by the children to find a comfortable place to stay and to ensure that they wouldn't be detected. Encourage student discussion of Claudia's choice for a bedroom, and suggest that they look at the map to find other appropriate places. Be sure they can give logical reasons for their choices.

7 Number students to form four teams. Give a chalkboard eraser, or other similar object, to the first person on each team. He must walk to the back of the line with the eraser on his head without dropping it. The eraser is then passed to the front and each succeeding person takes a turn. The team to finish first wins. After the game, ask why teams and teamwork are so important.

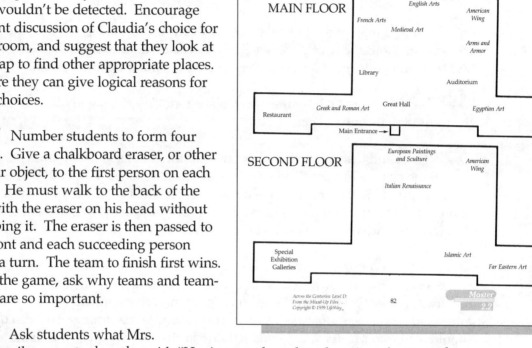

8 Ask students what Mrs. Frankweiler meant when she said, "Having words and explanations for everything is too modern." Does everything need to be explained? *(Sometimes things are better caught than taught and too much explanation muddles rather than clarifies.)* Direct their thinking to some Biblical examples of this concept.

- Psalm 8:3-5: David asks why God is mindful of human beings in light of all of the magnificence of His creation.

- Philippians 2:6-8: How can we explain why Christ was willing to become a mere human being and die for our sins in order that we might be reconciled to God and enjoy eternity in His presence?

- Daniel 4:25: Who can explain why God allows certain rulers and kingdoms to become powerful when they are wicked beyond measure?

9 Assign teams to gather information on the Italian Renaissance period. Assign the following topics: art, literature, scientific and mathematical discoveries, inventions, architecture, religion, medicine, government, Michelangelo and Leonardo da Vinci. Give them an appropriate time frame for this project and allow them to present their information in a variety of strategies: video, audiotapes, posters, TV interviews, team reports, etc.

10. Based on the amount of money Jamie had, and the amount they spent for their meal the first day, work with students to plan a budget for a week. Be sure to include a miscellaneous amount for unexpected expenses and save enough for train fare home. Check Chapter 1 for the amount needed. The budget should be compared with the expenditures made by Claudia and Jamie in subsequent chapters and revised as needed.

 **LESSON 3** (CHAPTER 4)

1 Vocabulary words may be introduced now or as they appear in the chapter.

2 Ask students to describe how Jamie and Claudia planned to move around undetected. How were these plans working out?

3 Give students the opportunity to discuss the daily activities Claudia and Jamie will have to plan and implement in order to make their adventure successful. List these on chart paper for future reference.

4 Ask students to think about Mr. and Mrs. Kincaid. Direct their thinking toward specific steps parents of runaway children would take. Use the following web example to brainstorm what these steps might be. Add other suggestions as they are made.

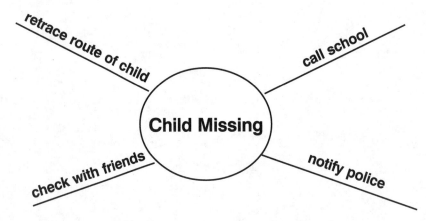

5 Read the first three pages of Chapter 4 and discuss the preparations the children made for the day.

6 Distribute copies of **Master 3.1** and review the directions. Students should keep this log throughout the rest of the book. They will fill in the information as directed. Extra pages may be added as needed.

7 Lead the class in discussing the following questions:

1) Why did Claudia decide they should choose a different gallery each day? Was this a good idea? Explain. *(She wanted to make sure they would learn while they were there. There was too much to learn to make her plan feasible.)*

2) What generally happens when people see a line in the general direction they are headed? Why? *(People instinctively join the line.)*

3) How did Jamie's choice, the Italian Renaissance, change the focus of the adventure? *(Claudia became enthralled with the beauty of the statue. When they became aware of the mystery involved, they now had a purpose and goal.)*

8 Continue reading until you reach the paragraph that gives the headlines, "Record Crowd Views Museum Bargain." Stop reading at the end of that paragraph. Ask students to predict what they think Claudia's reaction to the article will be. After discussing their predictions, complete reading the section that contains the account of the newspaper article. Allow students to refine their predictions of what they believe Claudia will do.

9 Read the article Claudia missed as she looked through the paper. Allow students to share what they think her reaction would have been and then to share what they think Jamie's reaction would have been. Direct them to explain their answers in terms of the personality characteristics they have already begun to observe in each child.

Claudia's Reaction	Jamie's Reaction
Claudia would be pleased with the description of herself as pretty.	*Jamie would probably want to go home.*

Across the Centuries: Level D: From the Mixed-Up Files . . .

10 Complete the chapter and continue discussion with the following questions:

1) How did Jamie's goal affect Claudia's thinking about their adventure? *(Claudia wanted to find out the solution immediately.)*

2) What do you think motivated Jamie to want to find who sculpted Angel? *(money)*

3) How did Claudia readjust her planning to incorporate Jamie's suggestion? *(She decided to limit the learning about everything and concentrate on Michelangelo.)*

4) What happened the second day that disappointed the children? How did they plan to compensate for this problem? *(The crowds caused the guards to hurry everyone past the statue. They decided to do their research when the museum was closed.)*

11 Claudia and Jamie appeared to join different school groups taking field trips to the museum. Assign students to write a paragraph in their literature journals about this decision. Direct them to answer the following questions in their paragraphs:

1) Why did Claudia and Jamie think it was important to be part of a group?

2) Why didn't the children in the groups they joined make a fuss or report them to a chaperon?

3) Why do you think they stayed with the group for lunch?

4) How would your class react to strange children joining your group on a field trip?

Below their paragraph, students can draw an illustration of Claudia and Jamie being near the group but never part of the group.

LESSON 4 (CHAPTER 5)

1 Introduce vocabulary now or as you come to it in the chapter.

2 Assign the first three pages of Chapter 5 for silent reading. After completion check students' understanding by discussing the following questions:

1) Why did Claudia insist on doing laundry? *(They changed underclothes each day and ran out of clean ones. She was brought up that way.)*

2) How does the phrase "Cleanliness is next to godliness" apply to Claudia? *(She liked things to be clean and to smell clean. She was passionate about clean.)*

3) What were the reasons the children chose Saturday to do their errands? *(There were no school groups in the museum on Saturday, and they would be more likely to be noticed.)*

4) How did they get their dirty clothes to the laundromat? Why did they choose this way? *(They stuffed what they could into their pockets and wore the rest over their clean clothes. They had no other way to carry them.)*

5) What were the results after the clothes were washed? Has this ever happened to you? Explain. *(Since everything was washed together in hot water, the colors faded, and everything turned gray.)*

6) How much did they spend? *(They spent $.55.)* How does this compare with the cost of the laundromat today? *(Check the cost of laundromats; most washing machines cost $1.00 to $1.50, and dryers cost $.25 for about 10 minutes.)*

7) How far did they walk to the library branch on 42nd Street? How far did they have to backtrack to get to the Donnell Branch? *(They walked approximately 40 blocks to the Main Branch Library and then had to backtrack about 11 blocks.)*

3 Soldiers use songs or chants to help them keep pace during long marches. Discuss how these help and ask students to share some they know. After sharing several, distribute copies of **Master 4.1** and have students work in pairs to write their own walking song or chant.

4 Read the next five pages together. Discuss the following questions:

1) Why did Claudia think she could become an authority on Michelangelo in one morning? *(She learned quickly; however, she didn't realize how much information there was to digest.)*

2) Compare Claudia's reasoning to students' reasoning in preparing for tests.

3) What did the author mean by the sentence, "Claudia showed the executive ability of a corporation president"? *(Claudia loved to plan and organize. She realized the task was huge, so she used the resources she had to divide the workload.)*

4) Why is delegating responsibilities essential to the completion of a group project? *(Each person has a valuable contribution to make. When each one does his part, the task is not left to just one or two. Everyone involved has a sense of accomplishment from seeing a job well done.)*

5) What, in the description of the library, lets you know that this book was written some years ago? *(The card catalog was used rather than computers for finding sources.)*

5 Display a transparency of **Master 4.2**, Organize for Success. Explain how the responsibilities are delegated. After students understand the principles, assign teams of four to design their own charts for the completion of a group project like planning a party or organizing a fund-raising activity.

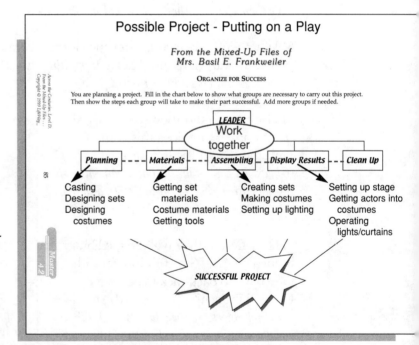

6 Display pictures or replicas of angels for the class to see.

1) Direct students to re-read Claudia's explanation of angels and cupids.

2) Give students the following Bible references to look up and read:
1 Chronicles 21:1-16; 2 Kings 6:17; Isaiah 6:1-4.

3) Ask students to compare these passages to Claudia's explanation and to the pictures and replicas of angels.

7 Divide the class into two debate teams to respond to this statement: It is all right to eat something you find on the ground, or that a stranger gives you, as long as it has a wrapper that is not torn. One team will take the affirmative and give reasons to support their position. The other team will take the negative and give reasons to show that this is not a good practice. (Suggest that students relate this to experiences with Halloween Trick-or-Treat candy.)

8 Direct students to read the next three pages silently. They are to pay close attention to the descriptive language the author uses, and find phrases that describe Jamie's feelings as he was waiting. Discuss their findings and reactions.

9 Assign the completion of the chapter. Review this section by asking the following questions:

1) What preparation did Claudia make for their bath earlier in the day? *(She scouted out the fountain area and took a supply of powdered soap and paper towels from the restroom so they could wash and dry themselves.)*

2) What made the bath worthwhile to Jamie? *(He found money that had been thrown into the fountain.)*

3) Why does the author say it is difficult to think in an organized way just before falling asleep? Is this true in your experience? Explain. *(Often when the mind and body are relaxed, thoughts seem to just come in random ways. We can't seem to focus on anything specific.)*

10 Hand out copies of **Master 4.3** and allow students to share their experiences with homesickness. Share that homesickness is a popular topic of poets because it is a common emotional experience. Discuss various styles of poetry and have the class dictate the first two lines of a poem about being homesick. The students can complete and illustrate the poem on the master.

LESSON 5 (CHAPTERS 6 AND 7)

1 Introduce the vocabulary as a group now or as you come to it in the text.

2 Assign the reading of Chapter 6. Guide discussion by asking the following questions:

1) What changes occurred in the children's schedule because it was Sunday? *(They slept later. They decided to go to the chapel and then explore.)*

2) What insight into their religious training does the chapel experience give you? *(They were used to going to church on Sunday.)*

3) Do you think Claudia was really sorry for stealing the paper? Explain. *(Probably not. Allow students to give their reasons.)*

4) How did the fact that it was Sunday cause the children to be careless? *(They had time to leisurely explore without anyone around. They forgot about the time because they were not on their regular schedule.)*

5) What discovery did they make on the old pedestal? *(They discovered the crushed mark on the velvet. It was a pushed-up M.)*

6) Where did they find the answer to the meaning of the mark? What did it mean? *(Jamie had noticed the same mark on the cover of one of the books he found at the library. They found the same book in the museum bookshop. It was Michelangelo's signature mark.)*

7) What slang expression does Jamie frequently use? *(Jamie's favorite slang expression was "Oh, baloney." This will become very important later in the story.)*

8) Why did Claudia say Angel was an answer to running away and also to going home again? *(They now had a purpose—a mystery to solve. Being able to solve the mystery would give a sense of accomplishment and closure to the adventure.)*

9) How did the children decide to let the museum authorities know about the clue? *(They decided to write an anonymous letter.)*

10) After reading Claudia's letter, how do you think museum officials will react? Explain. Have students spend time discussing this. How did the letter look? What was obvious about the way it was typed? What experiences have they had in sending letters to a business, government official, or some other adult organization? What kind of responses did they get?

3 Show several sculptures of angels, animals and people to students. Provide or have students bring clay, plasticene, mod-podge or other sculpting material. Demonstrate some techniques for using sculpting tools. These can include rosewood sticks, emery boards, plastic utensils or other kitchen utensils. Encourage students to design or mold a sculpture. Display the finished products in a prominent place.

4 Assign Chapter 7 for silent reading. After reading, assign teams of students to dramatize the following situations:

1) Jamie and Claudia renting the post office box
2) The encounter with Jamie's school class
3) Delivering the letter to the museum office

Allow students time to review their section, to rehearse their dialogue and to present their skit to the class. After the presentations, spend time in summarizing the lesson.

LESSON 6 (CHAPTER 8)

1 Introduce vocabulary as you read the chapter together.

2 Discuss the following questions:

1) How did Claudia and Jamie spend the time waiting for a response to their letter?

2) Have you ever had to wait for something? How did you feel? What did you do to make the time pass?

3) What was Jamie's story (tall tale)?

4) Do you think the ticket seller believed him? Explain.

5) Have you ever told a tall tale for being late, not having homework, not doing your chores? Was it believed? Share your experience.

3 Assign a research project. Claudia was searching for a way to be different. The girl dressed in traditional Indian costume was very distinctive. Assign teams to research the member nations of the United Nations then find details about their traditional dress and the culture it represents. Suggestions include India, China, Japan, Iran or any traditional Islamic country, Eastern European countries. Have them collect pictures for a collage or draw examples from their country of choice.

If desired, this activity can be incorporated into social studies and expanded to include a United Nations Festival with country reports, traditional dress, and an international dinner with a dish from each country.

4 Discuss the response of the museum officials. How did they treat the letter sent by Claudia and Jamie? *(They treated it with respect as if it had been written by a knowledgeable adult.)*

5 Complete discussion of this chapter by asking the following:

1) Why didn't Claudia want to go home? *(Nothing had happened to make her feel different.)*

2) What did Claudia mean in the statement, "I want to know how to go back to Greenwich different"? *(She wanted to feel important, to feel that running away had accomplished something.)*

3) What spur-of-the-moment decision did Claudia make? *(to go to see Mrs. Frankweiler)* Why was this unusual? *(Claudia usually planned everything in advance.)* Why did Jamie agree? *(He saw how important it was to Claudia.)*

6 Allow students to predict what will happen when the children reach Mrs. Frankweiler's home. Have them write their predictions on a card and hand them in. Keep them for later use.

LESSON 7 (CHAPTER 9)

1 Introduce vocabulary as a group now, or as terms are encountered in the text.

2 Read the first section of this chapter together. Stop reading at the place they go back to Mrs. Frankweiler's office after lunch. As an introduction to the chapter, have students:

1) Explain why Mrs. Frankweiler's office was such a total change from the rest of the house? *(Her office was like a modern laboratory. The rest of the house was filled with antiques.)*

2) Tell what Mrs. Frankweiler had been doing before she allowed the children to come in. *(She was doing research on the children. She called her lawyer, Saxonberg.)*

3) Speculate on why Mrs. Frankweiler called Saxonberg.

4) Demonstrate the kind of manner Parks had that would keep the children from interrupting. Allow two or three students to demonstrate this.

3 To summarize the rest of this section, assign teams to write questions for a "Meet the Press" type of discussion. Meeting the press will be Mrs. Frankweiler, Claudia and Jamie, and the children's parents. Questions should include the following topics:

1) Mrs. Frankweiler's activities prior to seeing the children
2) Claudia's audacious behavior in cleaning up
3) Jamie's inability to keep their hiding place a secret
4) Mrs. Frankweiler's bargain
5) The concern of the children's parents for their safety
6) Examples that demonstrated Mrs. Frankweiler's understanding of and fondness for Claudia and Jamie

After questions have been turned in, assign students to role-play those being interviewed, and two or three press interviewers to ask the questions. You may act as moderator or assign a capable student to that role.

4 Read the next four pages together and prepare a "Mind Map" similar to the one below to show the steps in the "Search for Solution to the Mystery."

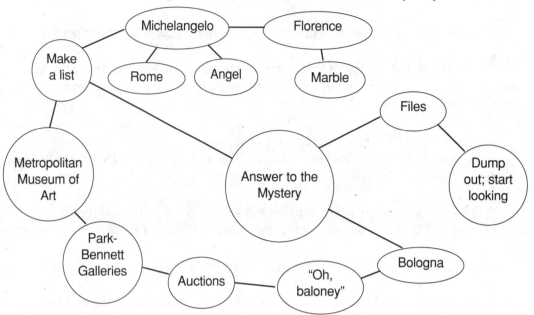

5 Illuminated manuscript writing was a highly developed art form during the Middle Ages. Provide copies of several examples for the students to study. Ask students to choose a favorite passage of Scripture to copy in this type of manuscript. Hand out copies of **Master 7.1** for them to complete their final work.

6 Return the students' predictions from the last chapter and compare them to what actually happened in this chapter.

7 Complete reading the chapter and discuss the following questions:

1) How did Mrs. Frankweiler obtain the sketch and why didn't she let the museum have it? *(She won it playing cards. She needed to have a secret more than she needed the money.)*

2) How did Mrs. Frankweiler ensure the children would not disclose the secret and Angel? *(She will leave the sketch to the children in her will. They will not get it until after she dies.)*

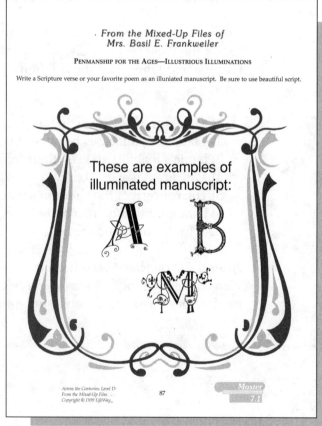

3) Have students find Jamie's reason for keeping the secret and then find Claudia's reason. *(Jamie will keep the secret because the sketch will be worth a lot of money. Claudia will keep the secret because just knowing it will make her important.)*

4) What did Mrs. Frankweiler mean about not learning anything new? Have them read from the book and then explain it in their own words.

8 Ask students to read Luke 15:3-7, the parable of the lost sheep. Discuss the role of the shepherd. How does the shepherd feel about that one lost sheep, even though there are 99 others? Does the number of sheep make a difference when one is missing?

Continue with Luke 15:11-24, the parable of the prodigal son. Relate this to Claudia and Jamie's running away?

1) How were they like the prodigal son?

2) How were they different?

3) Will their parents react the same as the father in the parable? Explain. What would your father's reaction be?

Hide a coin in the classroom. Tell students you have lost the coin and you need their help to find it. Provide several very general clues. After the coin has been found, read Luke 15:8-10 aloud. Ask students to relate this to Claudia and Jamie's experience. They sent a letter but gave no specific clues regarding their whereabouts.

9 If feasible, a team of volunteers could prepare a treasure hunt on the playground to teach the parable of the lost coin to younger students.

LESSON 8 (CHAPTER 10)

1 Introduce vocabulary, then read the first page and a half together.

2 Assign parts to students for reading the section in which Sheldon gives his report to Mrs. Frankweiler. Have students close their books at the end of that section.

3 Distribute copies of **Master 8.1**. Have students follow the directions to find the identity of the mystery person. *(Saxonburg)*

4 Direct students to finish reading the chapter.

5 Give out copies of **Master 8.2** and have students follow the directions to complete the acrostic describing Mrs. Frankweiler.

6 Ask students to speculate why Mrs. Frankweiler told Saxonberg he had better not tell the children that he has been her lawyer for 40 years. *(It has to do with keeping secrets.)*

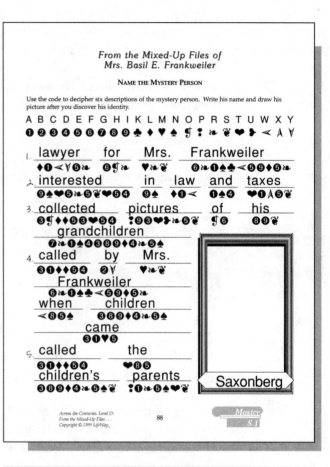

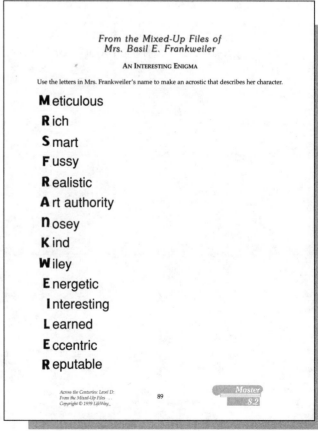

M eticulous
R ich
S mart
F ussy
R ealistic
A rt authority
n osey
K ind
W iley
E nergetic
I nteresting
L earned
E ccentric
R eputable

7 The children's stay at the museum had an unanticipated outcome that was very costly. Ask students what this was. Use this to open a discussion: What we do does not affect us alone. There are always unexpected effects, sometimes far reaching.

Draw a large fishbone on chart paper. (See **Master 8.3** for a pattern.) Have students fill in the bones as you discuss this issue.

8 Assign a written essay of half a page explaining ways in which what we do affects others and giving examples.

9 Distribute copies of **Master 8.4**. Read the directions together and let students work in pairs to complete the page.

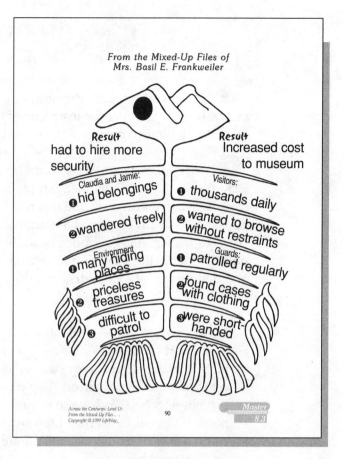

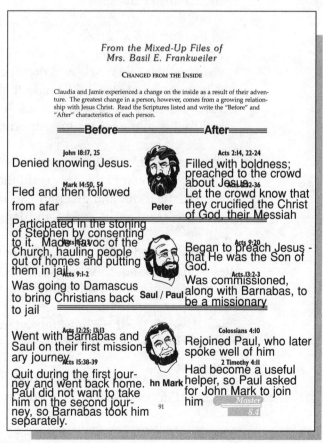

Enrichment

1 Design a Museum. Provide copies of **Master E.1**. Go over the instructions and allocate time to complete the projects.

2 Plan Your Work; Work Your Plan. Claudia was a careful planner. The success of the adventure was due in large part to her planning. God is the ultimate perfect planner. Assign groups or individuals to look up the following references and describe or illustrate/diagram the details of God's plan in each.

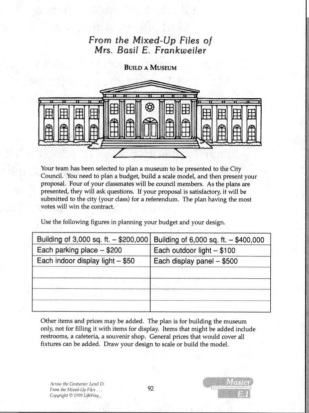

1) Genesis 1–2: Have students research and report on the natural laws (gravity, motion, matter and energy) that God set to govern the universe. They can explain why Earth is unique in supporting life. Students may plan and carry out demonstrations to illustrate these natural laws.

2) Exodus 25:8-27:21; 35:30-37:38: In addition to giving the details for constructing the Tabernacle and the Ark of the Covenant, what else did God do to make sure these were built exactly His way? Have students go back to Exodus 11:1-3 to find how God provided the Children of Israel with the means to support this project.

3) Numbers 2:10:11-28: Have students explain why order was so important in the arrangement of the camp and the march. Compare this to Mark 6:30-44 and then to the command given in 1 Corinthians 14:40. (You may use this to move the discussion to the need for order in the classroom and in the home.)

3 TV or Radio Talk Show. Students can pretend that Jamie and Claudia are guests on a talk show. Assign volunteers to develop a talk show interview with the children about their adventure, then videotape the interview.

4 Discuss the three most important lessons learned from the story. Write these on chart paper and display them in the classroom or in the library.

5 Student volunteers may write and perform a puppet play of a favorite part of the story. Puppets can then be made and the play presented for younger children.

6 Design a Web Page. If your school is on-line, students can design a Web page with interesting information, illustrations, excerpts from their character sketch activities, and biographical material about the author.

7 Create a Story Map. Assign teams to make a map of a specific section of the story. They should illustrate the location where their section is taking place and write two or three sentences describing the action. Tape the sections together to make a complete map of the story. This can then be used to tell the story to other classes and later placed in the library.

8 Plan a Museum Grand Opening. Feature the museum design projects and the various activities that were part of this unit. Invite school officials, other classes, parents and the local news media to the event. Refreshments can be planned, prepared and served by the students. This can be videotaped for later enjoyment.

9 Evaluation. Select an option for assessing students' achievement.

1) Choose one or two of the vocabulary activities to review and assess students' understanding.

2) Objective tests can be made by choosing questions from those listed in each lesson.

3) Various assignments completed during the unit can be accumulated into a portfolio for evaluation purposes.

4) Have students write a newspaper account of the return of Jamie and Claudia. Stress the differences in newspaper reporting and writing a research report.

5) Instruct students to create a cartoon strip or comic book that sequences the ten most important events in the story.

From the Mixed-Up Files of Mrs. Basil E. Frankweiler

MAGNIFICENT MUSEUM MEMORABILIA

On the left side of this chart list the kinds of exhibits that might be found in the museum you researched. On the right side list the source from which the museum may have obtained these exhibits. An example for an aerospace museum might be a space suit acquired from one of the early manned space flights.

_____
Name of Museum

Kind of Exhibit	Source of Exhibit

From the Mixed-Up Files of Mrs. Basil E. Frankweiler

WHAT A CHANGE OF SCENERY!

After reviewing information and pictures from a large metropolitan area like New York City, complete the Venn Diagram below. Write those things you would find in the large metropolitan area in the section on the left, things you would find in a small town on the right, and those things that could be found in both places in the middle.

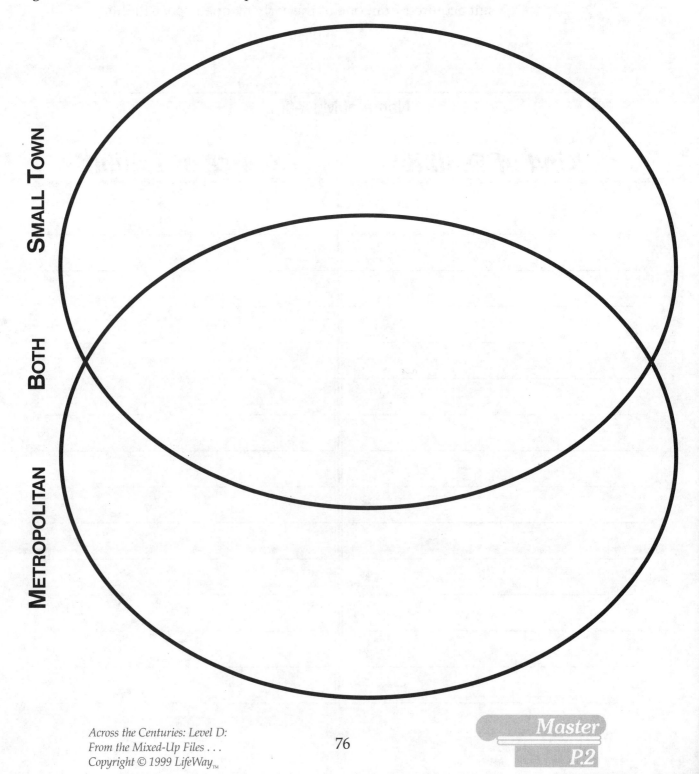

Across the Centuries: Level D:
From the Mixed-Up Files . . .
Copyright © 1999 LifeWay

From the Mixed-Up Files of Mrs. Basil E. Frankweiler

Vocabulary

Lesson One - Chapters 1 and 2

injustice
monotony
mah-jong
ventured
elegant
Manhattan
fiscal week
Neanderthal man
mutual
tycoon
boodle
percolator
commuters

Lesson Two - Chapter 3

extravagant
cheapskate
inconspicuous
matinee
Chancellor of the Exchequer
Marie Antoinette
ornately
alleged
fussbudget
English Renaissance
orthopedic shoes

Lesson Three - Chapter 4

automat
perilous
Italian Renaissance
impostors
embalm
acquisitions
Michelangelo
Prince Franz Josef II
curator
Bologna
hodgepodge
mediocre

Lesson Four - Chapter 5

laundromat
pagan
corpuscle
Mona Lisa
petit fours
espresso

Lesson Five - Chapters 6 and 7

stealthily
browsing
Congressional Medal of Honor
Rockefeller Center
Sistine Chapel
Mohammed
quarterly
drizzle
mastaba
familiarity

Lesson Six - Chapter 8

abrasions
sari
consensus
derby hat
counterfeited

Lesson Seven - Chapter 9

paupers
baroque
spigot
commotion
sauntered

Lesson Eight - Chapter 10

preoccupied
maimed
deceased
bequeathing

From the Mixed-Up Files of Mrs. Basil E. Frankweiler

YOU ARE APPRECIATED

Claudia decided to run away because she didn't feel appreciated. Write a note of appreciation to someone you think might feel like Claudia.

Cut out on dotted line, fold and send.

Across the Centuries: Level D:
From the Mixed-Up Files . . .
Copyright © 1999 LifeWay

From the Mixed-Up Files of Mrs. Basil E. Frankweiler

THE LADDER TO SUCCESS

If you are planning to do something special, you want it to be successful. Claudia wanted to make sure that her plans for this adventure were successful. Since she was a highly organized person, she planned carefully. Many plans depend on arranging details in a logical order. Make a five-step plan such as Claudia might have made. List each step on a rung of the ladder, beginning on the lowest with the one you believe should be first.

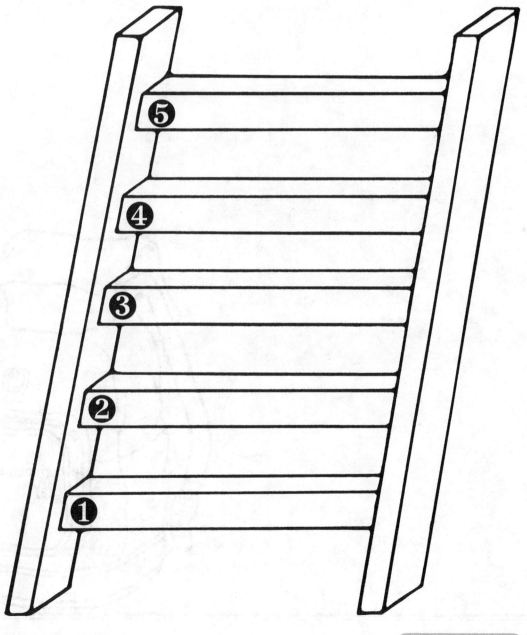

From the Mixed-Up Files of Mrs. Basil E. Frankweiler

PACK YOUR BAG

You are leaving tomorrow. You have only your backpack in which to pack everything you will need for a stay of one week. Draw those items that you will take. Don't forget essentials!

From the Mixed-Up Files of Mrs. Basil E. Frankweiler

Personality Profile

Because of their own unique personality characteristics, Claudia and Jamie responded differently to the situations they faced. Describe the way each responded to the situations listed. Find and list other situations and their responses as you read through the novel.

SITUATIONS

❶ Getting from Grand Central to the museum

❷ Choosing a place to eat

❸ Deciding how to spend the day

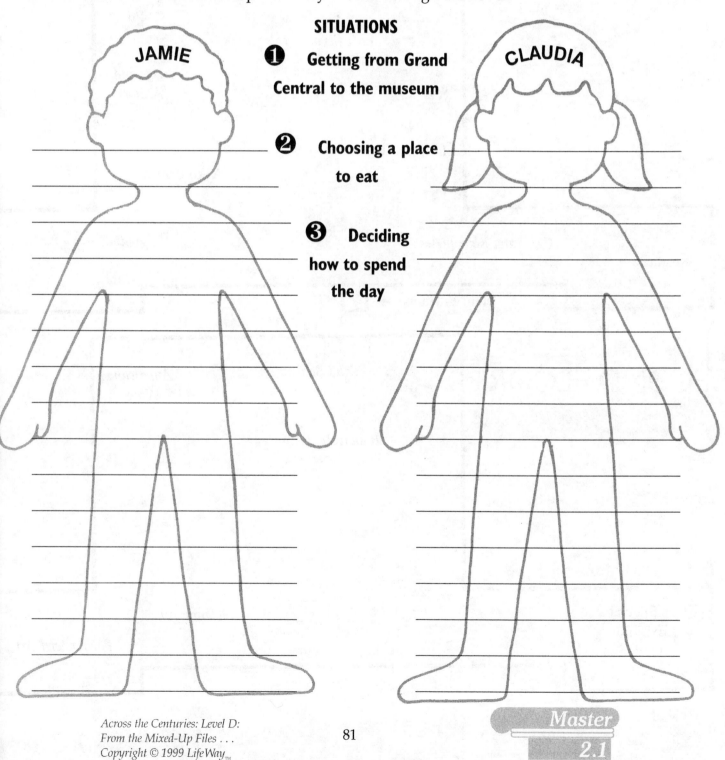

From the Mixed-Up Files of Mrs. Basil E. Frankweiler

MAP OF MUSEUM

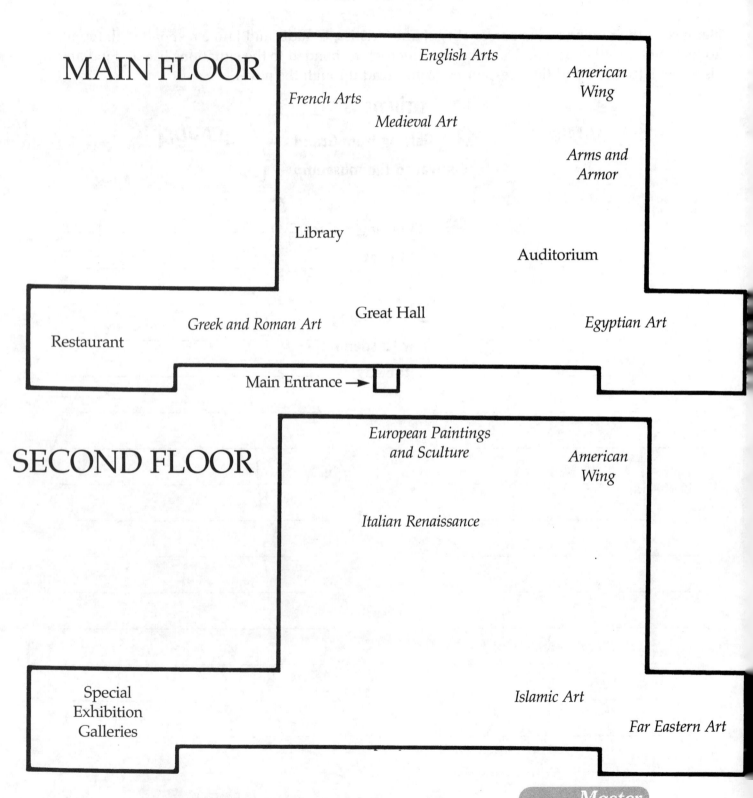

From the Mixed-Up Files of Mrs. Basil E. Frankweiler

Daily Doings Log

Keep a log of the children's daily activities while they are away from home. Write the day (Day One, Day Two) and the approximate time (morning, lunch, night). Describe the activity and make comments about it. See example.

Day	Time	Activity	Comments/Questions
Day One	Morning	They found places to hide their cases.	They couldn't carry them; they would be noticed if they checked them each day.

From the Mixed-Up Files of Mrs. Basil E. Frankweiler

AS WE GO MARCHING ALONG

Work with your partner to write a marching song or chant on the lines below.

Across the Centuries: Level D:
From the Mixed-Up Files . . .
Copyright © 1999 LifeWay

From the Mixed-Up Files of Mrs. Basil E. Frankweiler

Organize for Success

You are planning a project. Fill in the chart below to show what groups are necessary to carry out this project. Then show the steps each group will take to make their part successful. Add more groups if needed.

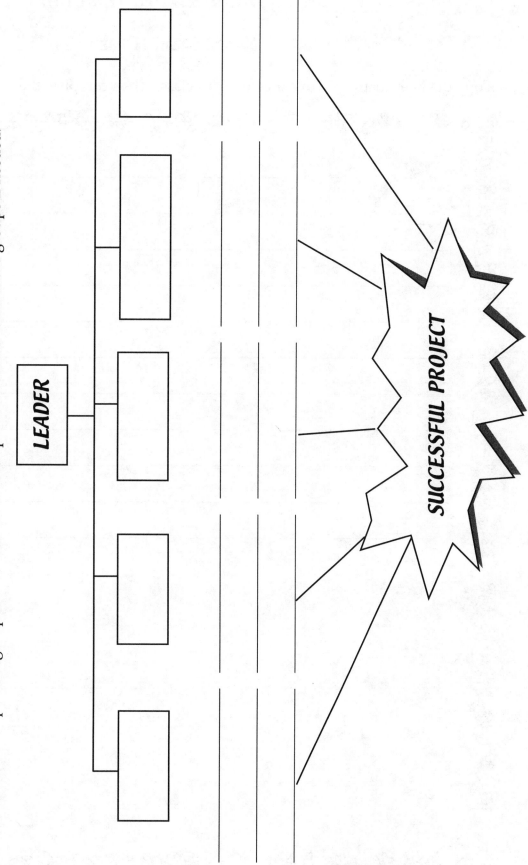

Across the Centuries: Level D: From the Mixed-Up Files . . . Copyright © 1999 LifeWay™

From the Mixed-Up Files of Mrs. Basil E. Frankweiler

HOME, SWEET HOME

Copy the lines that you wrote together as a class. Then complete the poem and illustrate it.

From the Mixed-Up Files of Mrs. Basil E. Frankweiler

PENMANSHIP FOR THE AGES—ILLUSTRIOUS ILLUMINATIONS

Write a Scripture verse or your favorite poem as an illuniated manuscript. Be sure to use beautiful script.

From the Mixed-Up Files of Mrs. Basil E. Frankweiler

NAME THE MYSTERY PERSON

Use the code to decipher six descriptions of the mystery person. Write his name and draw his picture after you discover his identity.

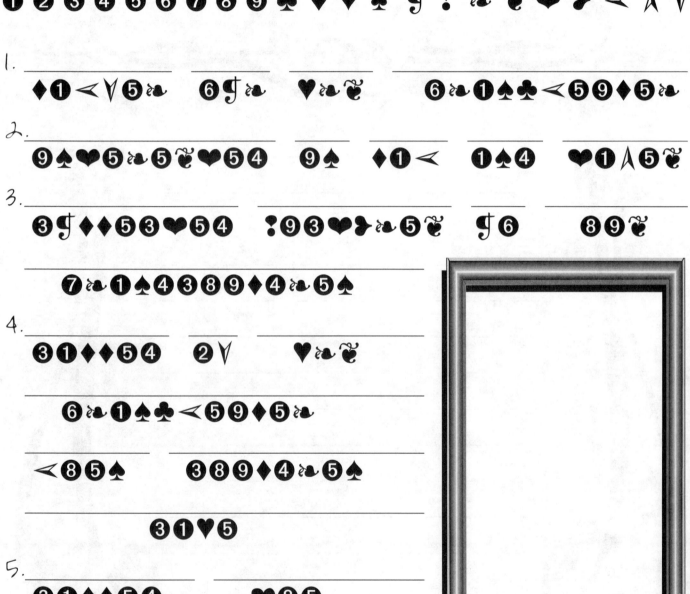

From the Mixed-Up Files of Mrs. Basil E. Frankweiler

AN INTERESTING ENIGMA

Use the letters in Mrs. Frankweiler's name to make an acrostic that describes her character.

M_____
R_____
S_____
F_____
R_____
A_____
N_____
K_____
W_____
E_____
I_____
L_____
E_____
R_____

Across the Centuries: Level D: From the Mixed-Up Files . . .
Copyright © 1999 LifeWay™

Master 8.2

From the Mixed-Up Files of Mrs. Basil E. Frankweiler

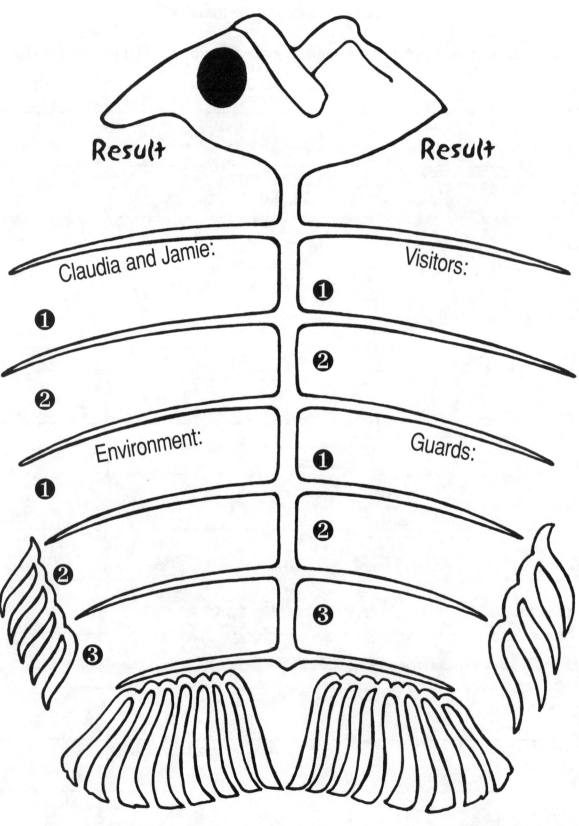

From the Mixed-Up Files of Mrs. Basil E. Frankweiler

CHANGED FROM THE INSIDE

Claudia and Jamie experienced a change on the inside as a result of their adventure. The greatest change in a person, however, comes from a growing relationship with Jesus Christ. Read the Scriptures listed and write the "Before" and "After" characteristics of each person.

═══Before═══   ═══After═══

John 18:17, 25   **Acts 2:14, 22-24**

Mark 14:50, 54   **Acts 2:32-36**

Peter

Acts 8:1, 3   **Acts 9:20**

Acts 9:1-2   **Acts 13:2-3**

Saul / Paul

Acts 12:25; 13:13   **Colossians 4:10**

Acts 15:38-39   **2 Timothy 4:11**

John Mark

From the Mixed-Up Files of Mrs. Basil E. Frankweiler

BUILD A MUSEUM

Your team has been selected to plan a museum to be presented to the City Council. You need to plan a budget, build a scale model, and then present your proposal. Four of your classmates will be council members. As the plans are presented, they will ask questions. If your proposal is satisfactory, it will be submitted to the city (your class) for a referendum. The plan having the most votes will win the contract.

Use the following figures in planning your budget and your design.

Building of 3,000 sq. ft. – $200,000	Building of 6,000 sq. ft. – $400,000
Each parking place – $200	Each outdoor light – $100
Each indoor display light – $50	Each display panel – $500

Other items and prices may be added. The plan is for building the museum only, not for filling it with items for display. Items that might be added include restrooms, a cafeteria, a souvenir shop. General prices that would cover all fixtures can be added. Draw your design to scale or build the model.

BLUE WILLOW
by Doris Gates

INTRODUCTION

The setting for Doris Gates' novel, *Blue Willow*, is the San Joaquin Valley in California during the Great Depression of the 1930s. The Larkin family gains strength and courage because of adversity. Students will admire them as an example of God's design for family relationships: loving headship of a father, loving submission of a mother and obedience given respectfully by their child.

OBJECTIVES:

1. Students will read and organize information from God's Word.

2. Students will write a story with a logical organizational pattern beginning with an introduction and including topic sentences, supporting paragraphs and a conclusion.

3. Students will design a picture to represent their story and paint it on a plate.

4. Students will incorporate information from library resources and web sites to use in charts, reports and on note cards.

5. Students will define and interpret idiomatic expressions.

6. Students will compare and contrast personalities in the story.

7. Students will elaborate the links between cause and effect.

SUMMARY OF STORY:

Blue Willow by Doris Gates tells the story of a migrant family during the Great Depression. Janey Larkin is ten years old and dreams of a house of her own. The one possession that makes her feel connected to a happier time is a blue willow china plate that was her great-great-grandmother's. As the Larkins settle in California's San Joaquin Valley, Janey meets Lupe Romero. For the first time, she allows herself to make a friend. *Blue Willow* is a heart-warming story of family. Students will admire the special kind of courage exhibited by Janey and her parents, who do what must be done without complaining.

PREPARATION:

1 Use *Dust For Dinner* by Ann Turner as an introduction to the plight of the prairie-land farmers during the Dust Bowl. Assign students to read a chapter at a time to the class. Share the illustrations and discuss the despair families experienced. Dorthea Lange and Walker Evans produced some award winning photography of migrant families. Display photographs of the era and allow students to sketch the photos.

2 Show a video about the Great Depression to give students visual images of the era. Let them search the community library and use the Internet to browse Web sites for information.

3 Provide cotton seeds for the class. Prepare a plot of land and plant the seeds in the early spring. Make arrangements for tending the crop over the summer. Assign volunteer students to keep journal information about the cotton plants until school is in session again. Bring the same students together in the fall to harvest the crop.

4 Discuss reasons why some families do not like to move frequently. Invite students to share some positive experiences they have had following a move.

5 Display pictures of automobiles from the 1930s. Ask students to draw and cut out a picture of one of them to use as a cover for a travel journal. Assemble a shape book by stapling pages of writing paper cut to fit behind the cover.

6 Have a family heritage day and invite students to bring photographs, family heirlooms, and also to dress in 1930–1940 style clothing.

7 Ask students to interview a grandparent or family friend who experienced the Great Depression. Have students videotape the interviews and share them with the class.

8 Distribute copies of the word search on **Master I.1** and pre-teach new vocabulary.

> Lesson 1 – Chapters 1-2: runty, arid, drought, rapt, incredulously, furtively, paltry
>
> Lesson 2 – Chapters 3-4: plaits, lustrous, sauntered, perplexed, aghast, rendered, jauntily, rivet, insolent, amiable
>
> Lesson 3 – Chapters 5-6: remonstrated, infinitesimal
>
> Lesson 4 – Chapters 7-8: blustering, tranquilly, dubious, vanquishing, disdainful
>
> Lesson 5 – Chapters 9-10: graft, jubilant, adobe

Implement one or more of the vocabulary activities:

1) Locate the vocabulary words in the text. Assign students to read the appropriate sentence and use context clues to define the word. Write these sentences on wall charts for later reference.

2) Distribute copies of **Master I.2** "Which Is Which?" Discuss the directions and assign it as independent work.

3) Divide the class into three or four groups. Direct two students per group to write each vocabulary word on an index card. Place the cards face down on the floor or table. Each player turns up two cards. If the cards match, he keeps them and tries again. If they do not match, they are turned back face down where they lie. The player with the most matching pairs wins the game. (Definitions may be used on one set of cards to add a level of difficulty.)

4) Distribute the words among the students. Direct the students to find three synonyms for their assigned words. Allow students a turn to attempt to get someone to say their word. They should use verbal clues including the synonyms listed.

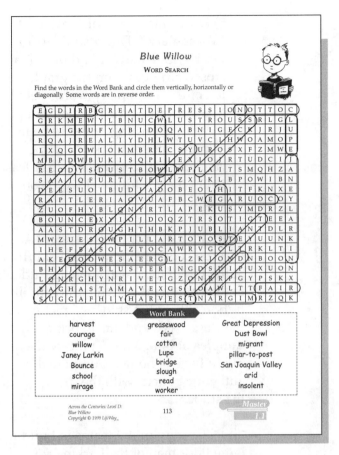

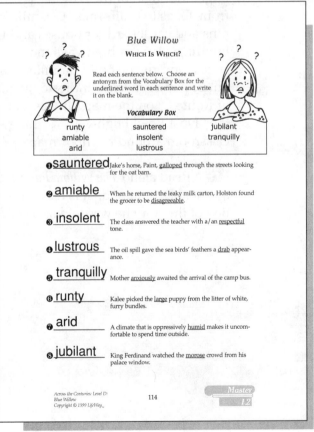

Across the Centuries: Level D:
Blue Willow

95

Copyright © 1999 LifeWay™

5) Distribute copies of **Master I.3** "Vocabulary." Direct students to work with a partner and design a crossword puzzle on the graph using ten of the vocabulary words listed. Make copies of the puzzles and place them in a learning center to be used as independent work. As a special challenge let students locate at least ten of these additional words on **Master 1.1**.

9 Pass out copies of **Master I.4**. Direct a choral reading of the old rhyme at the top of the page. Engage students in interpreting the rhyme through illustration. Share the students' pictures with the class. Ask students to bring any samples of blue willow pottery they might have at home. Compare the authentic pattern with the drawings of the students.

10 Guide student teams in building a large floor map of the Larkins' journey from Texas to California. Use milk cartons and cardboard for houses and tall buildings; lay out highways (no interstates) and rivers; build mountain ranges out of papier-mache. Indicate the path of Route 66 on the map. It was called the "Dust Bowl Highway." Arrange the classroom around the floor map.

11 Read aloud *The Willow Pattern Story*, by Allan Drummond. It is his own variation of the story he was told as a child.

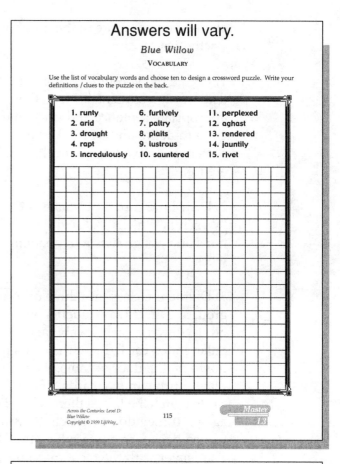

INSTRUCTIONAL PLAN

LESSON 1 (CHAPTERS 1 AND 2)

1 Introduce the novel with an explanation of the Great Depression and the Dust Bowl to familiarize students with the setting of the story.

2 Read Chapters 1 and 2. Guide a discussion using the following questions.

1) At the beginning of the story, readers discovered that Janey was not as tall as she should be. Discuss possible reasons for her being smaller than other children her age. *(genetic, frequent illness, poor nutrition, not enough food, hard work, poor appetite)*

2) Did Janey show evidence of having faith in God to provide for her family? Verify your answer. *(Yes. She believed Genesis 8:22 promised God's provision.)*

3) What did the author mean when she said Lupe spoke in a tone of exaggerated regret? *(Her reply was stressed with the intent to make Janey feel inferior.)* Choose two students to role-play this scene between Janey and Lupe. Remind "Lupe" to speak with exaggerated regret.

3 Distribute copies of **Master 1.1**. Instruct students to pack the car with the items needed to travel from place to place by drawing and labeling pictures inside and around the car. They may use Chapters 1-2 to find specific and inferred items. *(a few clothes, washboard, washtub, mattress, pillows, bedding, cooking utensils, eating utensils, gunnysacks, Bible, willow plate, suitcases)*

4 Review the story of Joseph (Genesis 37.) Guide a discussion comparing and contrasting Janey's lifestyle with Joseph's. *(They both were far from their homeland; both forced to take long journeys and live at the mercy of others; both were afraid and poor; both had faith in God; one was free, one was a slave; Joseph was alone and betrayed by his family; Janey moved with her family and was protected by their love.)*

5️⃣ Review with students the idea of writing from the first person point of view. Have them write in their travel journals Janey's thoughts about Lupe after their first meeting.

6️⃣ Divide the class into small groups. Use research materials including the Internet to discover what effect the influx of immigrants into California had on the residents of the state. Have each group put their findings on chart paper and display the charts from the ceiling. *(decreased available jobs, put extra burden on relief agencies, increased possibility of epidemics, created overcrowding)*

7️⃣ Choose two students (or two dads) to dramatize the role of candidates for governor of California during the Depression. Prepare opposing platforms about the immigrants. Assign students to make campaign posters. Assign campaign managers to write speeches of introduction. Divide the class into newspaper reporting teams. Hold a press conference with the two candidates. Have the newspaper reporting teams develop and ask the questions. Each team will choose one of the candidates and write an article of endorsement for the newspaper represented. Print the articles and choose newsboys to deliver the papers to other classes.

8️⃣ Require students to write a creative story in their travel journals using the blue willow plate story as a pattern. They should keep the story simple with clear descriptions of the characters, setting, statement of conflict, and resolution.

9️⃣ Distribute copies of **Master 1.2**. Students are to design a plate to represent their story. When they are satisfied with their design, allow them to paint it on a white plastic plate.

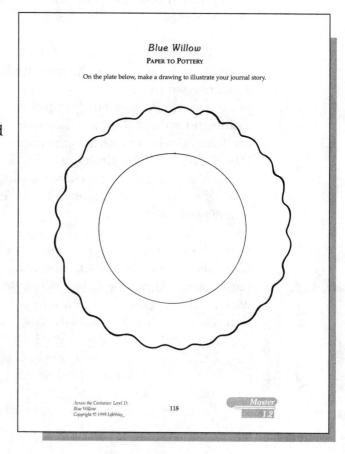

Alternate activity: If possible, take a field trip to a ceramic shop where students can paint bisque plates and have them fired.

🔟 Have students illustrate their interpretation of the inside of the Larkins' shack.

11 Solve the following problems using mental math:

1) Mr. Larkin was paid two "bits" an hour to work in the cotton fields. He worked eight hours a day. Janey figured out that he made two dollars a day. How much is two "bits"? *(25 cents)*

2) What would he make in a day if he were paid double time for eight hours? *($4.00)*

3) Suppose Mr. Larkin worked for two full weeks, including Saturdays and Sundays. If he made $4.00 a day, how much would he make in the two weeks. *($56.00)* How much would he make in one week? *($28.00)*

4) If the Larkins were asked to pay $5.00 rent each week and Mr. Larkin made $14.00 per week, how much would be left to buy food and other necessary items? *($9.00)*

5) Mr. Larkin was not paid if he could not work. Suppose he injured himself and was unable to work for three days. How much money would he bring home that week? *($8.00)*

6) His rent remained $5.00 a week. Now what was left to buy food? *($3.00)*

7) Would it be possible today to feed and clothe a family of three people on $14.00 per week? *(No)* Why? *(The prices of goods and services are much higher today.)*

12 Choose a student to read aloud Colossians 3:18–21. Distribute copies of **Master 1.3** and direct students to read and follow the directions.

13 Distribute copies of the quiz on **Master 1.4** to evaluate Lesson 1.

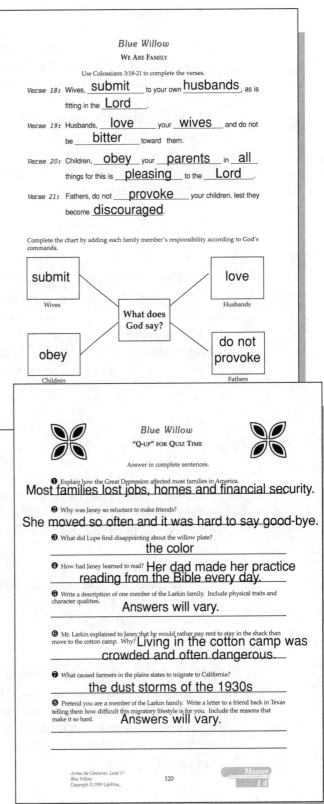

Across the Centuries: Level D:
Blue Willow

Lesson 2 (Chapters 3 and 4)

1 Ask students to browse through Chapter 3.

1) What exciting thing may happen in this chapter? *(a trip to the fair)*

2) Make a list of clue words on the board that give the reader that impression. *(fair, an arch marked Entrance, Ferris wheel, race track, livestock, booths, prize, exhibits, stage, magician, merry-go-round, brass ring)*

3) Ask students to make predictions about the kind of character Bounce Reyburn will be.

2 Read Chapters 3 and 4. Lead the class in a discussion of the chapters using the following questions.

1) What change did Janey notice in her mother's attitude as she dressed for the fair? *(She looked happy, less tired, and gave Janey a nickel to spend.)*

2) Why did Janey's trip please Mrs. Larkin? *(Janey was doing something special for the first time. Her mother was happy for her.)*

3) Even with the excitement of the fair, Janey had an underlying feeling of insecurity. Why did she feel that way? *(never being sure how long she would stay in one place)*

4) What impressed Janey most at the fair? *(the library booth)*

5) What caused a misunderstanding between Janey and Lupe at the fair? *(Janey was unaccustomed to having friends and thought Lupe felt sorry for her.)*

6) Why was Mr. Larkin indignant toward Bounce Reyburn? *(He thought Bounce Reyburn was rude and was suspicious of his intentions.)*

3 Distribute copies of **Master 2.1** regarding idiomatic expressions. Then challenge students to collect idiomatic expressions and post them with literal and figurative illustrations on the bulletin board.

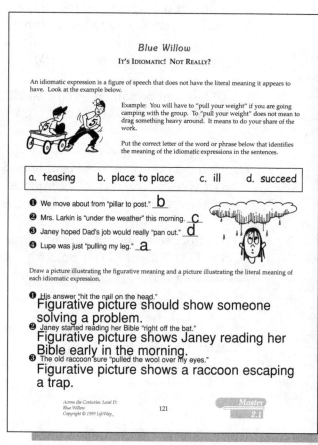

Across the Centuries: Level D: Blue Willow

100

Copyright © 1999 LifeWay™

4 Distribute copies of **Master 2.2**. Discuss the directions to be certain students can make an accurate comparison.

5 Direct students to write and illustrate shape books. Suggested topics: Trucks, Flowers, Dogs, Horses, Butterflies. The cover and pages should be the shape of the topic. Display the books around the room and invite a kindergarten class to come for story time. Allow kindergartners to choose a book and an older student to read it to them. Send the books with the kindergartners to put in their classroom library.

6 Choose several students to read Numbers 13 aloud from their Bibles. After spying out the land, what did the men bring back to the people to show the bounty of Canaan? *(a branch with one cluster of grapes carried between them on a pole; pomegranates and figs)* What did Janey bring back to her parents? *(eggs)*

> **Blue Willow**
> "In the sweat of your face you shall eat bread." (Genesis 3:19)
>
> Use the Venn diagram to compare and contrast Mr. Larkin's job with the principal's job at your school.
>
> **Possible answers:**
>
> Mr. Larkin: worked outdoors, physically strenuous, changes locations often, poorly paid, no days off with pay
>
> School Principal: works indoors, has an office, works more with people, must have a college degree
>
> Both: require responsibility and honesty, a need to be flexible
>
> (Accept any reasonable answers.)
>
> Use drawing paper and design an employment advertisement for one of the following positions. Include qualifications necessary, hours, location and other pertinent information to attract potential employees. Choose one: bank teller, brick mason, fashion designer, fireman, Pony Express mail carrier, baseball coach, photographer, hospital cook.

7 Choose two students to dramatize the roles of a newspaper reporter and Bounce Reyburn. Have the reporter interview Mr. Reyburn in a way that will expose his character to the newspaper readers. Give students time to write a headline that would be appropriate to appear with the interview. Print banner headlines on the computer and display them around the room. (Example: Bouncer Reyburn to Bounce Small Fry and Family)

8 Janey and her family enjoyed a picnic together by the river. Have students draw a picture of the picnic, putting in dialogue balloons for each character and writing some thoughts each one might have as they spend special time together.

9 Divide the class into four groups to review Chapters 1-4. Assign each group a chapter. Distribute copies of **Master 2.3** "The Main Events." When completed, compile the information from each group on one large chart to display in the room.

1) Upon completion of **Master 2.3**, students will each illustrate one event from their group's assigned chapter.

2) Arrange illustrations in sequential order.

3) Choose one student from each group to narrate the group's chapter.

Blue Willow
THE MAIN EVENTS

Working in groups, list the main events of the chapter assigned.

Chapter 1:
1) Larkins arrived in San Joaquin Valley.
2) Janey met Lupe Romero.
3) Janey told Lupe about the willow plate.
4) Janey made her first friend.

Chapter 2:
1) Mrs. Larkin cleaned the shack and began to prepare dinner.
2) Janey read her daily lesson from the Bible and expressed her faith that God would always provide for them.
3) Mr. Larkin came home at sundown.
4) Janey talked with Dad about how long they could stay.

Chapter 3:
1) Lupe invited Janey to the Fresno County Fair.
2) Mrs. Larkin gave Janey a nickel to spend at the fair.
3) Janey discovered the library booth.
4) Janey and Lupe had a misunderstanding.

Chapter 4:
1) Bounce Reyburn demanded money for rent.
2) The Larkins went on a picnic by the river.
3) Janey went exploring and found the Anderson ranch.
4) Bounce Reyburn accused Janey of attempting to steal from the ranch, but she was befriended by Mr. Anderson.

Across the Centuries: Level D:
Blue Willow
Copyright © 1999 LifeWay

Master 2.3

LESSON 3 (CHAPTERS 5 AND 6)

1 Before reading Chapter 5, ask students to predict what the camp school might be like. Write the predictions on the board. *(crowded, hot, everyone from different places, children not the same ages)*

2 Place each student with a partner and have pairs read Chapters 5 and 6 together, alternating pages. Use the following questions for class discussion.

1) How did Janey plan to test the teacher? *(She planned to show her the toad to see what she would call it.)*

2) Miss Peterson suggested Fafnir as a name for the toad. Was that a good choice? *(Yes)* Why? *(She thought he looked like a dragon named Fafnir who had lived in days gone by.)*

3) What name would you have picked for the horned toad?

4) According to Mr. Larkin, how was their family life like an adventure? *(They did not know what to expect from day to day.)*

5) Discuss ways Mr. Larkin demonstrated proper Biblical leadership for his family while they were shopping. *(He looked for a bargain on the tires, kept track of the spending, took them out to eat as a treat, bought Janey a much needed coat, managed to return home with some money left, etc.)*

6) Choose a student to narrate the cotton picking contest event. *(They should include Janey's excitement during the preparation, the prizes, Mr. Larkin's helper, winners.)*

7) Enact what the camp school was like with the class.

3 Distribute copies of **Master 3.1** "School Daze" and discuss the directions before assigning its completion.

4 Display pictures of horned toads in the classroom, directing students to draw a picture of the animal. Ask students to find five facts about the horned toad and put them in a brief report with illustrations. Bind the reports together to make a book for the classroom library.

5 Have a "Terrific Toad Day" in the classroom. Ask each student to bring a garden toad or lizard from their yard in a box with the toad's name printed on the outside. Display the animals in the classroom for the day. Distribute copies of **Master 3.2** and discuss the directions together. Warn students that some species of toads are poisonous and should be avoided.

6 Distribute copies of **Master 3.3**. Display completed book covers in the hall or in the school library.

7 Re-read and discuss the shopping trip into Fresno. Have students draw a map of the town square, putting in the places the Larkins stopped. They can summarize in two or three brief sentences what happened at each location.

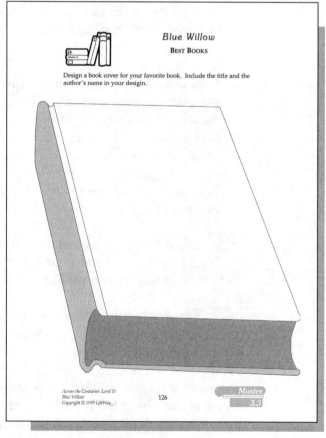

8 Distribute copies of **Master 3.4** and make a transparency to use for demonstration. Guide the class in using the formula given to compare prices. Arrange a field trip to a farm or a farmer's market where students can purchase fruits and vegetables.

9 Plan a cotton picking contest for the students if a crop is ready for harvest. An alternate activity is to have a field day. Allow the class to decide on events to include. (three-legged races, cotton sack races, painting cotton T-shirts, relay races)

10 Distribute copies of **Master 3.5** "A Different Kind of Courage." Discuss the directions with the class and assign it as an independent activity. An open-minded portrait is an illustration using the outline of the character's head. Pictures are drawn within the shape to show the thoughts of the character as directed in the explanation.

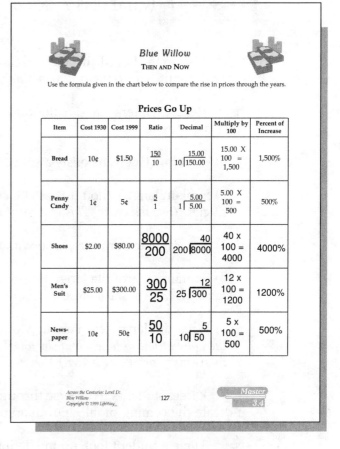

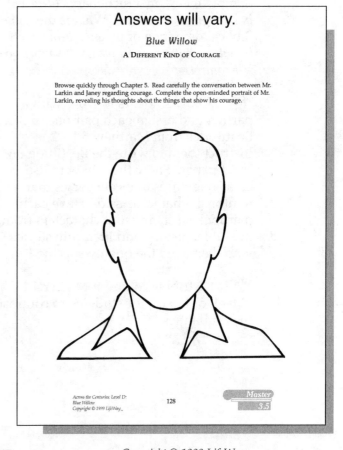

Lesson 4 (Chapters 7 and 8)

1 List on the board situations that could occur to make the Larkins' life more difficult. *(car trouble, illness, no work available for Mr. Larkin)*

2 Read Chapters 7 and 8 aloud to the class. Use the following questions for a class discussion.

1) What had Janey anxiously awaited? *(the arrival of the ducks at the slough)*

2) Explain Janey's thoughts as she crouched near the slough to watch the ducks. *(She thought, "This is what it means to inherit the earth.")*

3) According to Scripture, who will inherit the earth? *(the meek, Matthew 5:5)*

4) Explain the trouble Janey found while at the slough. *(She saw Bounce Reyburn there to shoot ducks.)*

5) What did Janey learn about Mom and the willow plate? *(Mom knew what the plate meant to Janey, and she loved it too. Sometimes we must let something go to discover something better.)*

3 Direct students to browse through Chapter 7 and look for clue words that indicate the coming of fall. Put them on a chart entitled "Fall Is Here."

4 Have a student look up the definition of "meek" in a dictionary. *(deficient in strength and courage)* What is the Biblical definition of meek? *(being gentle in nature, but strong in the Lord; having good self-control)*

5 Allow students to work with a partner and assign each pair one of the Beatitudes from Matthew 5:1–12. Instruct them to write the Beatitude on chart paper. Show them how to use cross-references to locate verses that reinforce what Jesus said. Have each pair make a short list of characters from the Bible, history, and literature stories who displayed the quality specified.

6 Distribute copies of **Master 4.1** "Meek or Weak" for students to contrast these qualities.

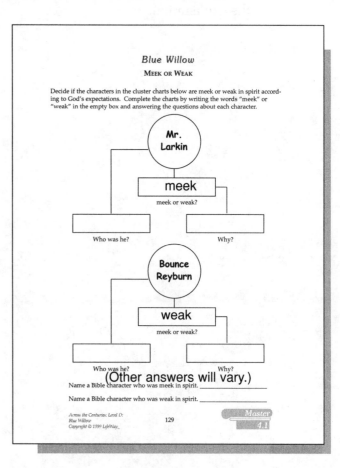

Across the Centuries: Level D: Blue Willow

7 Look up "slough" in the dictionary. *(small body of water with deep mud and mire; swampy)* Read to the class Chapter 4, "The Slough of Despond," from *Little Pilgrim's Progress*, by Helen L. Taylor. When we find ourselves in difficult situations, sometimes we can fall into the "Slough of Despond." Distribute copies of **Master 4.2** "Slippery Slough." Discuss the directions and assign as an independent activity.

8 Ask a student to draw a large outline of Bounce Reyburn on butcher paper. Put the figure on a bulletin board or wall. Choose students to tell about specific events that showed him to be the antagonist. Allow students to write the events on the figure.

9 Distribute copies of **Master 4.3** to use as an evaluation tool.

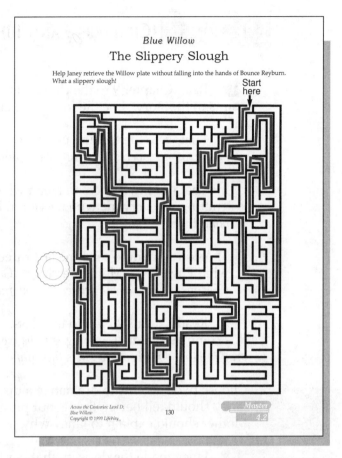

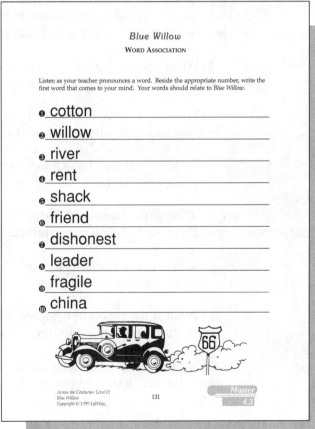

Across the Centuries: Level D: Blue Willow

LESSON 5 (CHAPTERS 9 AND 10)

1 Read Chapter 9 to the class. Instruct students to listen for two turning points in the story. Use the following questions to lead the class in discussion.

1) What were the turning points in this chapter? *(Dad's decision to leave. Mr. Anderson discovered the truth about Bounce Reyburn.)*

2) What did Mr. Anderson mean when he said Bounce had "probably been grafting on everyone who moved in here"? *(He had gotten money from them dishonestly.)*

3) Ask a student to read the last three paragraphs of Chapter 9 to the class. To what Power was Mom referring? *(God)* What did Janey do "just to be safe"? *(She offered up a silent prayer to God and to the willow plate.)*

2 Read Exodus 20:1–3 to the class. Guide a discussion about the meaning of this commandment. *(Nothing is to be more important in our lives than God. We are to pray to Him alone because He is the only one who has power to answer prayers.)*

Choose two students to dramatize a discussion between Janey and her mother. Janey should tell her mother about praying to the willow plate "just to be safe." Mother should explain to Janey why, as Christians, we only need to pray to God.

3 Janey made the decision that her family was more important than the willow plate. Twice she was willing to give it up to keep them out of harm's way. Direct students to choose one of the following related writing activities.

1) Write a paragraph about a time when you had to give up something to make things better or more convenient for your family.

2) Write a paragraph describing Dr. Pierce. Discuss his character qualities, his personality and why you think he would not take the willow plate from Janey.

3) Pretend you are Bounce Reyburn. Write a note to the Larkins explaining how they can be sure the willow plate is returned.

4 Distribute copies of **Master 5.1** "Happily Ever After." Direct students to write their own ending to the novel.

5 Choose two students to read Chapter 10 to the class by alternating pages. Discuss the following questions.

1) What is the mood of Chapter 10? *(joy)* Choose students to read passages from the chapter to verify the mood.

2) Should Janey have been allowed to put the willow plate on display in the tank-house? Explain your answer. *(Accept answers that exhibit reasonable thinking.)*

Across the Centuries: Level D:
Blue Willow

3) Direct students to describe or draw a picture of what Janey saw when she opened the door of the new house.

6 Use copies of **Master 5.2** to compare and contrast student endings with that of the author.

7 Bring closure to the novel by guiding a discussion about priorities. Assist in bringing out the point that relationships should always be a higher priority than things. Although Janey connected her happiness to the willow plate, the love of God and of her family were the real basis for her joy. Ask students to locate Bible verses that demonstrate God's love for people rather than material goods. *(John 3:16; 2 Corinthians 8:9; Galatians 5:14; John 15:12)*

8 Distribute copies of **Master 5.3** to use for evaluation of the novel.

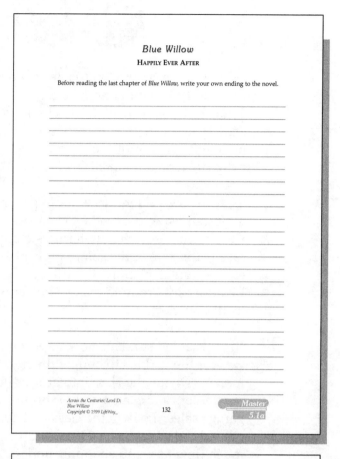

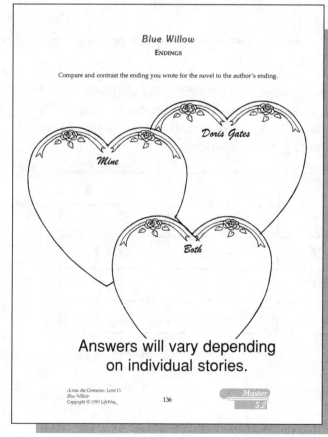

ENRICHMENT

1 Put the activity on **Master E.1** on a chart and place it in a science center. Send students in small groups to do the activity and make observations to determine how grass roots hold down topsoil better than an unplanted field.

2 Allow students to work in groups to design ways to prevent soil erosion. Have them research how farmers today take better care of the soil to prevent erosion and depletion of nutrients. Require each group to make a poster of its discoveries.

3 Remind students how important it was for the Larkins to budget their money. Divide the class into groups of four or less and plan a day to shop garage sales. Look in the classified ads of the local newspaper. Decide how much time to spend shopping and choose three or four sales. Number the sales and use the following chart as an example to schedule the groups to avoid overcrowding. Ask parents to drive. Students should have a designated amount to spend, a list of items to purchase, a copy of the schedule, a street map and a list of addresses for the garage sale locations. When students return to school, have them share their purchases. Discuss who found the best bargains and which sale had the most interesting merchandise.

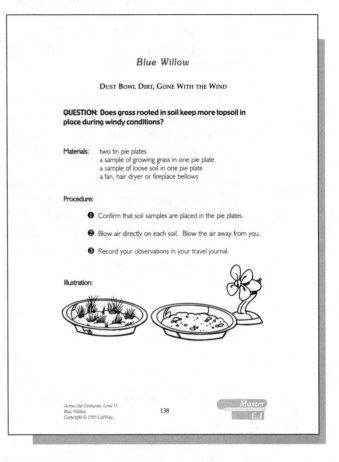

	Group 1	Group 2	Group 3	Group 4
9:00	Sale 1	Sale 1	Sale 1	Sale 1
9:30	Sale 2	Sale 2	Sale 2	Sale 2
10:00	Sale 3	Sale 3	Sale 3	Sale 3
10:30	Sale 4	Sale 4	Sale 4	Sale 4

4 Build a King Cotton Museum. Direct students to research topics related to the cotton industry. They can work in pairs or small groups to collect information from the Internet, encyclopedias, CDs, and libraries, then make charts and displays. Have students serve as tour guides, reciting the information presented. Invite parents and other classes to visit the museum. Suggested topics for research: Eli Whitney, the cotton gin, history of cotton as a cultivated plant, planting, harvesting, pests such as the boll weevil and the pink bollworm, spinning cotton into yarn, uses of cotton seeds, the importance of cotton to the South during the 1800s, life on cotton plantations, changes in cotton farming today.

5 Read to the class excerpts from *King Arthur and His Knights* by Sir James Knowles, *Little Pilgrim's Progress* by Helen L. Taylor, or *Pilgrim's Progress* by John Bunyan. Let students discuss the positive character qualities that can result from experiencing hardships. Read 1 Peter 1:6–7 and James 1:2–3 as part of the discussion.

6 Locate a school or children's home in need. Have students decorate shoe boxes and fill them with school supplies such as pencils, crayons, glue sticks, scissors, rulers, markers, tablets and story books, and deliver them to the chosen location. Discuss the importance of the items being new.

7 Invite parents to come for lunch and serve an enchilada meal like Mrs. Romero would prepare. Decorate the room with 1930s furniture, plates, table cloths. Play 1930s music. Have the students dress up in 1930s clothes. Present student narrations of *Blue Willow*, a chapter at a time. Prepare appropriate scenery panels for each chapter to use as background while the students recite.

8 Place students into groups and have them develop questions and ideas for a *Blue Willow* board game.

9 Most families escaping the Dust Bowl traveled on Route 66. Assign research projects to discover the historical significance of the highway. Allow students to collect and bring any memorabilia they can find to share with the class. If part of Route 66 is close enough, plan a field trip along the highway. Stop along the way to talk to merchants and citizens.

10 Locate information about Cesar Chavez and the National Farm Workers Association. Lead a class discussion to familiarize students with his concerns and the concerns of the farm owners. Have half of the class design posters calling for fair wages and better living conditions for workers and their families. The remaining half may design posters taking the point of view of the farm owners. Invite another class to join the group and serve as mediators to help negotiate a contract between the workers and owners.

11 Read some Norse myths to the class. Discuss Fafnir the Dragon and where he fits into Norse mythology.

Across the Centuries: Level D: Blue Willow

RESOURCES:

Durmmond, Allan. *The Willow Plate Story*. Harper Collins Publishers, 1995.

Dust Bowl Science. Frank Schaffer Publications, Inc. 1996.

Georgano, Nick. *The American Automobile: A Centenary*. Smithmark Publishers, New York, NY, 1992.

Turner, Ann. *Dust for Dinner*. North-South Books, New York, 1992.

Web site - http://www.best.com/sfmuseum/hist8/ok.html

Web site - http://lcweb2.loc.gov./ammem/afetshtml/tshome.html

Web site - http://nutmeg.ctstateu.edu./depts/edu/textbooks/dustbowl.html

Web site -http//www.pbs.org/wgbh/pages/amex/dustbowl/eyewitness.html

Blue Willow
WORD SEARCH

Find the words in the Word Bank and circle them vertically, horizontally or diagonally Some words are in reverse order.

E	G	D	I	R	B	G	R	E	A	T	D	E	P	R	E	S	S	I	O	N	O	T	T	O	C
G	R	K	M	E	W	Y	L	B	N	U	C	W	L	U	S	T	R	O	U	S	S	R	L	G	L
A	A	I	G	K	U	F	Y	A	B	I	D	O	Q	A	B	N	I	G	F	C	K	J	R	J	U
R	Q	A	J	R	E	A	L	I	Y	D	H	L	W	T	U	V	C	I	H	W	O	A	M	O	P
I	X	Q	G	O	W	I	O	K	M	B	R	L	C	S	Y	U	R	O	S	X	F	Z	M	W	E
M	B	P	D	W	B	U	K	I	S	Q	P	I	L	E	X	I	O	J	R	T	U	D	C	I	J
R	E	O	D	Y	S	D	U	S	T	B	O	W	L	W	P	L	A	I	T	S	M	Q	H	Z	A
S	A	A	J	Q	F	U	R	T	I	V	E	L	Y	Z	X	L	K	L	B	P	O	W	I	B	N
D	E	E	S	U	O	I	B	U	D	J	A	D	O	B	E	O	L	H	I	T	F	K	N	X	E
R	A	P	T	L	E	R	I	A	O	V	U	A	F	B	C	W	E	G	A	R	U	O	C	O	Y
Z	U	O	F	H	Y	B	L	Q	N	Y	R	T	L	A	P	E	K	U	S	Y	M	D	R	Z	L
B	O	U	N	C	E	X	Y	I	O	J	D	O	Q	Z	T	R	S	O	T	I	G	T	E	E	A
A	A	S	T	D	R	O	U	G	H	T	H	B	K	P	J	U	B	L	I	A	N	T	D	L	R
M	W	Z	U	E	S	Q	W	P	I	L	L	A	R	T	O	P	O	S	T	E	Y	U	U	N	K
I	H	E	F	B	A	S	O	L	Z	T	O	C	A	W	R	V	G	C	L	T	R	K	L	T	I
A	K	E	D	O	O	W	E	S	A	E	R	G	L	L	Z	K	J	O	N	D	N	B	O	O	N
B	H	U	J	Q	O	B	L	U	S	T	E	R	I	N	G	D	S	U	I	P	U	X	U	O	N
L	Q	N	R	G	H	Y	N	R	I	V	E	T	G	Z	O	N	R	R	P	G	Y	P	S	K	X
E	A	G	H	A	S	T	A	M	A	V	E	X	G	S	I	O	A	W	L	T	T	F	A	I	R
S	U	G	G	A	F	H	I	Y	H	A	R	V	E	S	T	N	A	R	G	I	M	R	Z	Q	K

Word Bank

harvest	greasewood	Great Depression
courage	fair	Dust Bowl
willow	cotton	migrant
Janey Larkin	Lupe	pillar-to-post
Bounce	bridge	San Joaquin Valley
school	slough	arid
mirage	read	insolent
	worker	

Across the Centuries: Level D:
Blue Willow
Copyright © 1999 LifeWay™

113

Blue Willow

Which Is Which?

Read each sentence below. Choose an antonym from the Vocabulary Box for the underlined word in each sentence and write it on the blank.

Vocabulary Box

runty	sauntered	jubilant
amiable	insolent	tranquilly
arid	lustrous	

❶ _____ Jake's horse, Paint, <u>galloped</u> through the streets looking for the oat barn.

❷ _____ When he returned the leaky milk carton, Holston found the grocer to be <u>disagreeable</u>.

❸ _____ The class answered the teacher with a/an <u>respectful</u> tone.

❹ _____ The oil spill gave the sea birds' feathers a <u>drab</u> appearance.

❺ _____ Mother <u>anxiously</u> awaited the arrival of the camp bus.

❻ _____ Kalee picked the <u>large</u> puppy from the litter of white, furry bundles.

❼ _____ A climate that is oppressively <u>humid</u> makes it uncomfortable to spend time outside.

❽ _____ King Ferdinand watched the <u>morose</u> crowd from his palace window.

Across the Centuries: Level D:
Blue Willow
Copyright © 1999 LifeWay

Blue Willow

VOCABULARY

Use the list of vocabulary words and choose ten to design a crossword puzzle. Write your definitions/clues to the puzzle on the back.

1. runty
2. arid
3. drought
4. rapt
5. incredulously
6. furtively
7. paltry
8. plaits
9. lustrous
10. sauntered
11. perplexed
12. aghast
13. rendered
14. jauntily
15. rivet

Blue Willow

RHYME THYME

Illustrate the rhyme below.

Two pigeons flying high
Chinese vessel sailing by
Weeping willow hanging o'er
Bridge with three men, if not four.
Chinese temples there they stand
Seem to take up all the land,
Apple trees with apples on,
A pretty fence to end my song.

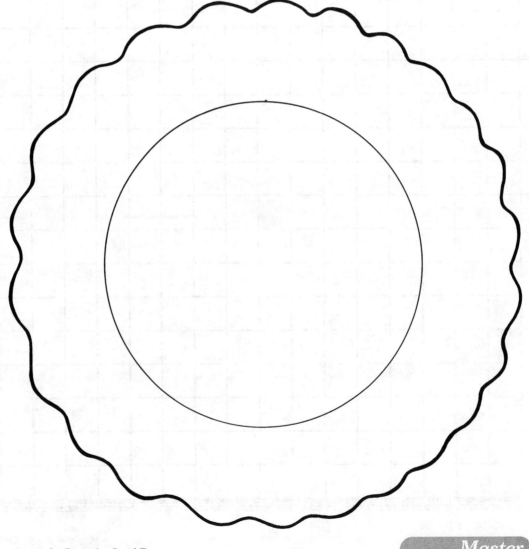

Across the Centuries: Level D:
Blue Willow
Copyright © 1999 LifeWay

Master
I.4

Blue Willow
PACK UP YOUR TROUBLES

Around and on the car below, draw and label items the Larkins carried with them to set up housekeeping in the camps.

Blue Willow

PAPER TO POTTERY

On the plate below, make a drawing to illustrate your journal story.

Across the Centuries: Level D:
Blue Willow
Copyright © 1999 LifeWay™

Master 1.2

Blue Willow

WE ARE FAMILY

Use Colossians 3:18-21 to complete the verses.

Verse 18: Wives, _____ to your own _____, as is fitting in the _____.

Verse 19: Husbands, _____ your _____ and do not be _____ toward them.

Verse 20: Children, _____ your _____ in _____ things for this is _____ to the _____.

Verse 21: Fathers, do not _____ your children, lest they become _____.

Complete the chart by adding each family member's responsibility according to God's commands.

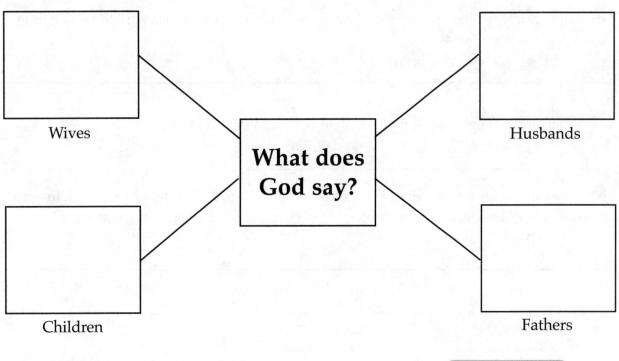

Blue Willow

"Q-UP" FOR QUIZ TIME

Answer in complete sentences.

❶ Explain how the Great Depression affected most families in America.

❷ Why was Janey so reluctant to make friends?

❸ What did Lupe find disappointing about the willow plate?

❹ How had Janey learned to read?

❺ Write a description of one member of the Larkin family. Include physical traits and character qualities.

❻ Mr. Larkin explained to Janey that he would rather pay rent to stay in the shack than move to the cotton camp. Why?

❼ What caused farmers in the plains states to migrate to California?

❽ Pretend you are a member of the Larkin family. Write a letter to a friend back in Texas telling them how difficult this migratory lifestyle is for you. Include the reasons that make it so hard.

Blue Willow

IT'S IDIOMATIC! NOT REALLY?

An idiomatic expression is a figure of speech that does not have the literal meaning it appears to have. Look at the example below.

Example: You will have to "pull your weight" if you are going camping with the group. To "pull your weight" does not mean to drag something heavy around. It means to do your share of the work.

Put the correct letter of the word or phrase below that identifies the meaning of the idiomatic expressions in the sentences.

---

a. teasing   b. place to place   c. ill   d. succeed

---

❶ We move about from "pillar to post." ____

❷ Mrs. Larkin is "under the weather" this morning. ____

❸ Janey hoped Dad's job would really "pan out." ____

❹ Lupe was just "pulling my leg." ____

Draw a picture illustrating the figurative meaning and a picture illustrating the literal meaning of each idiomatic expression.

❶ His answer "hit the nail on the head."

❷ Janey started reading her Bible "right off the bat."

❸ The old raccoon sure "pulled the wool over my eyes."

Blue Willow

"In the sweat of your face you shall eat bread." (Genesis 3:19)

Use the Venn diagram to compare and contrast Mr. Larkin's job with the principal's job at your school.

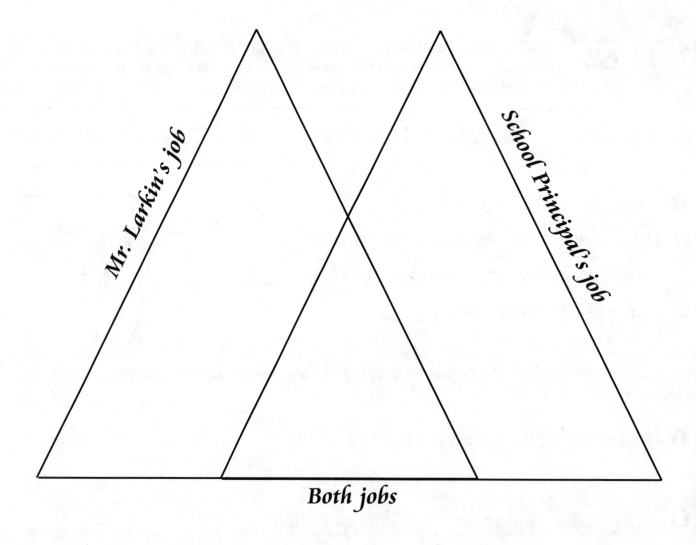

Use drawing paper and design an employment advertisement for one of the following positions. Include qualifications necessary, hours, location and other pertinent information to attract potential employees. Choose one: bank teller, brick mason, fashion designer, fireman, Pony Express mail carrier, baseball coach, photographer, hospital cook.

Blue Willow

The Main Events

Working in groups, list the main events of the chapter assigned.

Chapter 1:

1) _____
2) _____
3) _____
4) _____

Chapter 2:

1) _____
2) _____
3) _____
4) _____

Chapter 3:

1) _____
2) _____
3) _____
4) _____

Chapter 4:

1) _____
2) _____
3) _____
4) _____

Blue Willow

SCHOOL DAZE

If Janey Larkin were a new student in your class, how would she be treated? What could these people say to her to make her first day easier?

If you were a new student, what are some things you would like for people to do for you on your first day? _____

_____

What would be the hardest adjustment to make as a new student? _____

_____

Blue Willow

Write a story to reflect the title below. Use rebus pictures for the nouns in your story.

Mr. Toad Goes to School

Blue Willow
BEST BOOKS

Design a book cover for your favorite book. Include the title and the author's name in your design.

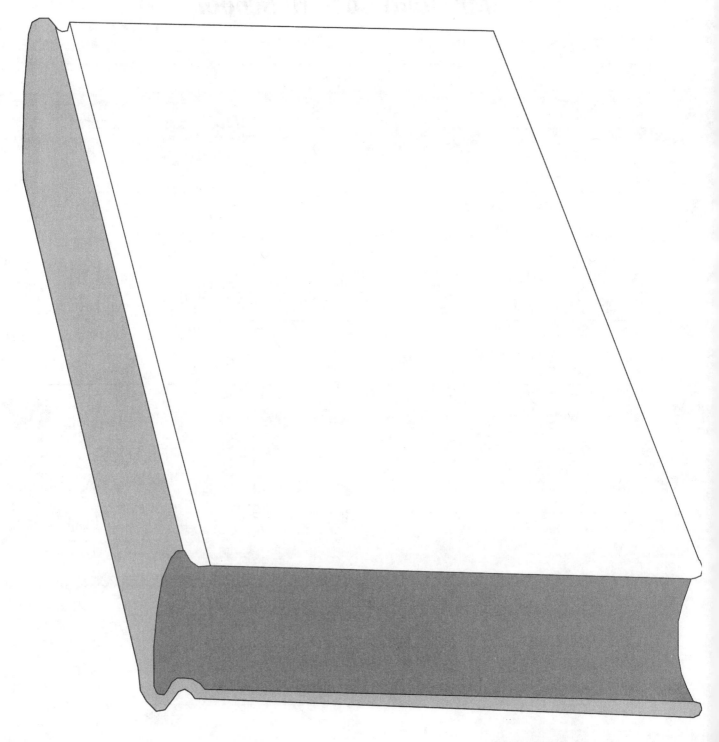

Blue Willow

Then and Now

Use the formula given in the chart below to compare the rise in prices through the years.

Prices Go Up

Item	Cost 1930	Cost 1999	Ratio	Decimal	Multiply by 100	Percent of Increase
Bread	10¢	$1.50	$\frac{150}{10}$	$10\overline{)15.00 \atop 150.00}$	15.00 X 100 = 1,500	1,500%
Penny Candy	1¢	5¢	$\frac{5}{1}$	$1\overline{)5.00 \atop 5.00}$	5.00 X 100 = 500	500%
Shoes	$2.00	$80.00				
Men's Suit	$25.00	$300.00				
News-paper	10¢	50¢				

Across the Centuries: Level D:
Blue Willow
Copyright © 1999 LifeWay™

Master 3.4

Blue Willow

A Different Kind of Courage

Browse quickly through Chapter 5. Read carefully the conversation between Mr. Larkin and Janey regarding courage. Complete the open-minded portrait of Mr. Larkin, revealing his thoughts about the things that show his courage.

Blue Willow

MEEK OR WEAK

Decide if the characters in the cluster charts below are meek or weak in spirit according to God's expectations. Complete the charts by writing the words "meek" or "weak" in the empty box and answering the questions about each character.

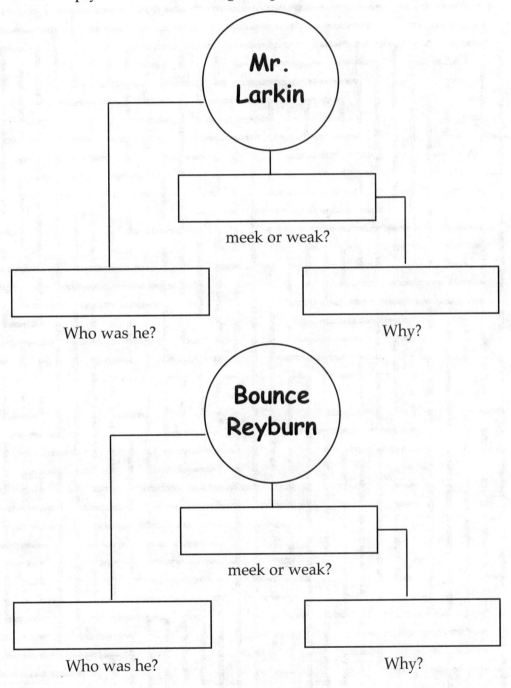

Name a Bible character who was meek in spirit. _____

Name a Bible character who was weak in spirit. _____

Blue Willow

THE SLIPPERY SLOUGH

Help Janey retrieve the Willow plate without falling into the hands of Bounce Reyburn. What a slippery slough!

Blue Willow
WORD ASSOCIATION

Listen as your teacher pronounces a word. Beside the appropriate number, write the first word that comes to your mind. Your words should relate to *Blue Willow*.

❶ _____

❷ _____

❸ _____

❹ _____

❺ _____

❻ _____

❼ _____

❽ _____

❾ _____

❿ _____

Blue Willow

HAPPILY EVER AFTER

Before reading the last chapter of *Blue Willow,* write your own ending to the novel.

_____
_____
_____
_____
_____
_____
_____
_____
_____
_____
_____
_____
_____
_____
_____
_____
_____
_____
_____
_____
_____
_____
_____

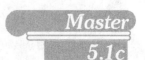

Blue Willow

ENDINGS

Compare and contrast the ending you wrote for the novel to the author's ending.

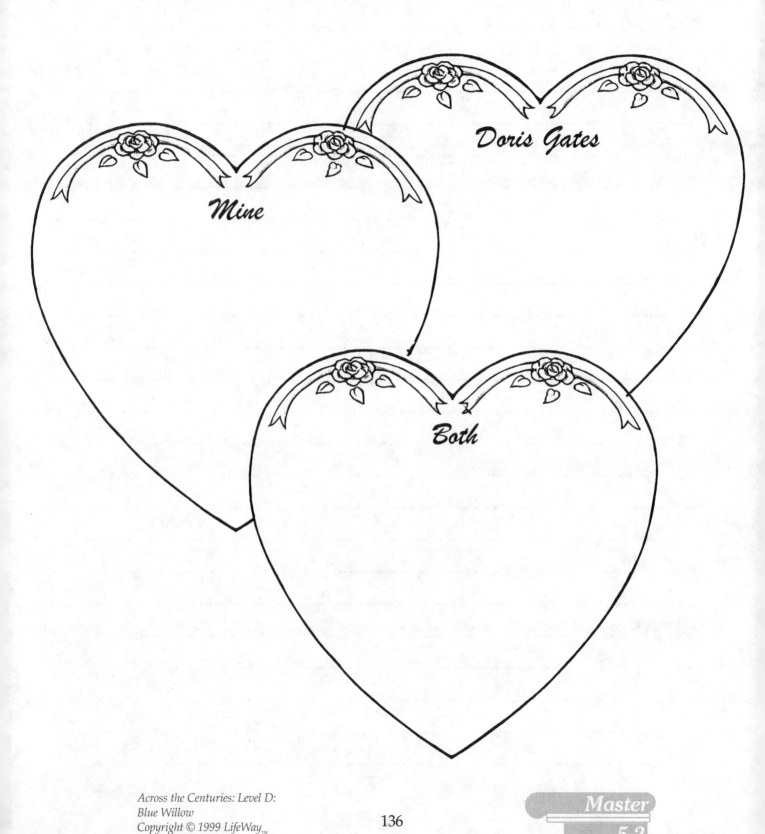

Blue Willow

EVALUATION TIME

Complete one of the following projects.

1 Make paper dolls of the main characters in the novel and write descriptions of their character traits on the back of each one.

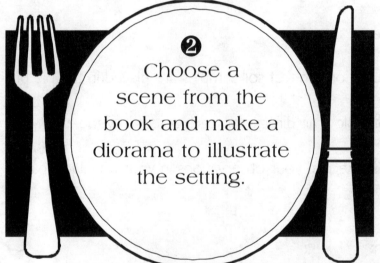

2 Choose a scene from the book and make a diorama to illustrate the setting.

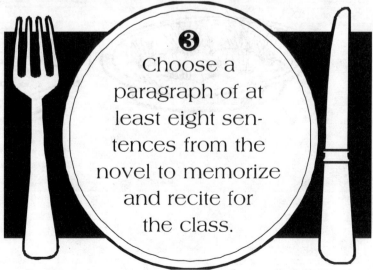

3 Choose a paragraph of at least eight sentences from the novel to memorize and recite for the class.

Blue Willow

Dust Bowl Dirt, Gone With the Wind

QUESTION: Does grass rooted in soil keep more topsoil in place during windy conditions?

Materials: two tin pie plates
a sample of growing grass in one pie plate
a sample of loose soil in one pie plate
a fan, hair dryer or fireplace bellows

Procedure:

❶ Confirm that soil samples are placed in the pie plates.

❷ Blow air directly on each soil. Blow the air away from you.

❸ Record your observations in your travel journal.

Illustration:

CALL IT COURAGE

by Armstrong Sperry

INTRODUCTION

Call It Courage is a novel that will encourage students to face their fears in order to become stronger individuals. It is the story of Mafatu, a Polynesian boy, who lived long ago on the island of Hikueru in the South Pacific. He is the son of the Great Chief and is expected to be a source of pride for his father. His people value courage above all attributes, but Mafatu is shamed because he fears the sea. Readers are swept along with Mafatu as he determines to overcome his fear or leave his home forever. As students see how Mafatu fears the wrath of his pagan gods, they should be reminded of the loving God who empowers them with His own strength to overcome fear. His promise to never leave us is a wonderful source of comfort as students face the challenges of life.

OBJECTIVES:

1 Students will use appropriate reference materials to gather information about the history of the Polynesian culture, information about coral environments and the formation of hurricanes and tropical storms.

2 Students will compare and contrast island formations in the Pacific.

3 Students will determine from information provided in the text the steps in building a model of an outrigger canoe.

4 Students will describe the effect of ocean currents on small sailing vessels in the open sea.

5 Students will explain the Scriptural truths of the following statement: "Christ is the Bread of Life."

6 Students will compare the story of Mafatu to "the Prodigal Son."

7 Students will write paragraphs with a topic sentence and three supporting sentences.

SUMMARY OF STORY:

Mafatu is a Polynesian boy whose name means Stout Heart. His name is an embarrassment because the villagers think he is a coward. As a young child, Mafatu accompanied his mother in a canoe to look for sea urchins. As a hurricane approached, his mother lost control of the canoe. They were washed out to sea. His mother was killed and he was left alone until rescued. Fear of the sea follows Mafatu like a dark shadow. His father, the Great Chief of Hikueru, is shamed by his son's refusal to fish with the other boys of the island. The people of the island value courage and have no tolerance for fear. Mafatu leaves the island, not to return until conquering his fear of the sea. Living in humiliation before his father is harder than facing his self-imposed enemy, the sea.

ABOUT THE AUTHOR:

Armstrong Sperry was born in New Haven, Connecticut, in 1897. He spent much of his childhood listening to his great-grandfather tell stories of his adventures as a sailor in the South Pacific. He became fascinated by the South Pacific and lived there for a short time. Sperry showed an early interest in art and worked in commercial art before becoming an author and illustrator of children's books. He illustrated many of his own books. His historical fiction provides readers with a splendid view of times gone by. His young heroes develop strength and character in exciting stories. Armstrong Sperry received the Newbery Medal in 1941 for *Call It Courage*. He died in 1976.

Other books written and illustrated by Armstrong Sperry:
Little Eagle, A Navajo Boy; Philadelphia, Winston
Lost Lagoon; Doubleday
Coconut, The Wonder Tree; MacMillan
Bamboo, The Grass Tree; MacMillan
No Brighter Story; MacMillan
The Rain Forest; MacMillan

Oceania: Oceania refers to an area in the central and south Pacific encompassing widely scattered groups of islands. Some of the islands are large landmasses such as New Guinea. Others are small atolls with few inhabitants. All of the Oceania islands have volcanic bases submerged deep below the sea. Oceania is divided into three main island groups: Melanesia (in the Southwest), Micronesia (in the Northwest) and Polynesia (in the East).

Polynesian Islands: In *Call It Courage*, Mafatu and his people were native to the Polynesian Islands. They were an agricultural society. The islands, mostly small atolls, were historically divided into family groups, with the chieftain being in command of the entire group. He was usually the eldest son in a line of eldest sons.

The Black Islands: The islands of Melanesia were also called the "black islands." It is possible that these were the Smoking Islands that Mafatu was warned about by his grandfather. This area in the Pacific is the setting in the novel, *Call It Courage*.

Preparation:

Choose from the following activities to prepare students for the study of *Call It Courage*. Use the activities to familiarize students with tropical locations and to develop an awareness of other cultures.

1 Write to the Bishop Museum in Honolulu, Hawaii, and request historical information available about the history of the Polynesian people. Address: Bishop Museum, 1525 Bernice Street, Honolulu, Hawaii 96817-0916, USA

2 Divide the class into small groups or pairs and research these islands of Polynesia: Hawaii, New Zealand, Tahiti, Cook Islands, Tonga, Samoa, Easter Island, Midway Island. Ask the groups to prepare five to ten trivia questions to present interesting information to the entire class.

3 Discuss how students would prepare for an ocean voyage in a small sailing vessel. Have the students make personal checklists needed before the trip could begin.

4 Researching the Pacific Oceania, ask students to design a wall mural of the area including the island groups of Melanesia, Micronesia and Polynesia. Add population figures, products, distances and major tourist attractions.

5 One of the themes of the book is overcoming personal fears. Allow students to voluntarily discuss some of their own fears. Explain how fears can develop from certain situations. Share a childhood fear from your own background.

6 Pre-teach some of the new vocabulary words students will encounter.

> Lesson 1 (Chapter 1): Polynesians, barrier reef, impending, millrace, frigate, outrigger, thwart, capsize, pinnacle, pandanus, scorn, nondescript, sennet, taut.
>
> Lesson 2 (Chapter 2): atoll, convulsively, ominous, oppressive, cachalot, ballast, squall, frothing, wrought, hewn, marrow, rending, tumult, slewed.
>
> Lesson 3 (Chapter 3): giddy, ghost-terns, congealed, cauterize, caustic, liana, plateau, circumference, shoaled, basalt, ramparts, polyp, impaled, adze, extricated, irresolute, premonition, grotesque, convolvulus, writhed, famished.
>
> Lesson 4 (Chapter 4): buoyant, imperative, perilous, oblique, phosphorescent.
>
> Lesson 5 (Chapter 5): tattoo, interstellar, zephyr, riptide, gracile, conflagration, benign, nautilus, iridescence.

7 Implement several of the following vocabulary activities.

1) Design a Polynesian class glossary with illustrations of each vocabulary word.

2) Encourage students to invent vocabulary board games to use at the beginning of each chapter.

3) Instruct students to write a synonym for the following vocabulary words: taut, scorn, ominous, giddy, caustic, famished, grotesque, imperative, buoyant, benign.

4) Make a word chart with the following categories: The Sea, Island Life, Weather, Landforms.

5) Provide books, CD-ROMS, encyclopedia and Internet access for classroom research on sea life, islands of the Pacific, the Pacific Rim nations, volcanoes and monsoons.

8 Instruct students to build a Captain's Sea Log for the study of *Call It Courage*. Have students keep the glossary, chapter notes and writing assignments in the Sea Logs. **Master I.1** can be duplicated for this purpose. The students can decorate the cover of a folder in which to place the log sheets.

Instructional Plan

Lesson 1 (Chapter 1): Flight

1 Discuss the mural or a map of Oceania. Note the distance between the three areas: Melanesia, Micronesia and Polynesia. Ask the students to use graph paper to draw maps of Oceania to scale.

2 Polynesians are noted for their expertise in sailing and canoe design. Select students to search for pictures of the Polynesian outrigger canoe. Divide the class into groups and instruct each group to design and build a model of an outrigger canoe. Enlist the assistance of parents to help put the models together in class.

3 Read Chapter 1, "Flight." Use the following questions to discuss the chapter.

1) Mafatu's people believed in many gods. Moana, the sea god, was a continual threat to Mafatu. Why? *(Mafatu escaped death in the hurricane that killed his mother. He believed Moana still desired his death.)*

2) Moana was forever changing. He was calm one moment and angry the next, dashing upon the island in his thunderous rage. How does he compare to the one true God who loves us? *(God is a living God in whom we can trust. He will never change. He will remain the same tomorrow as He is today.)*

4 Tell students to locate Psalm 145:13-16 in their Bibles. Ask a student to read the verses aloud to the group. Teach students to use the concordance in their Bibles to locate other verses that speak of God's faithfulness to His own. *(Lamentations 3:23, Psalm 117:2, Isaiah 11:5 are examples.)*

5 Make a mini-book.

1) Distribute copies of **Master 1.1**. Require students to find information from the Media Center about coral and coral reefs.

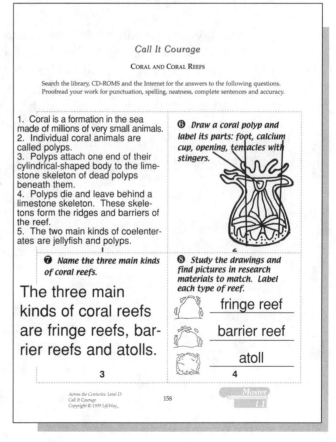

Across the Centuries: Level D: Call It Courage

2) Using copies of **Master 1.2**, students are to illustrate four kinds of coral.

3) Distribute copies of **Master 1.3** and make a transparency of it. As you fill in the blanks for discussion using the overhead projector, instruct the students to fill in the blanks on their copy.

4) Direct students to cut out the boxes on the dotted lines of **Masters 1.1, 1.2** and **1.3**. Students should design a cover for their books and bind the pages together to make a mini-book.

6 Provide the class with various building materials and instruct them to design a model of a coral reef in the classroom. Allow them to work in small groups, using the research information to add plants and animals that inhabit the reef environment. Encourage students to be creative in their choice of supplies. Invite other classes and parents to view the finished project.

7 As an evaluation tool, direct students to write a paragraph in their Captain's Sea Logs explaining how they would prepare for an ocean voyage in a small sailing vessel such as an outrigger canoe. Paragraph points should include ideas discussed in class during the preparation for reading.

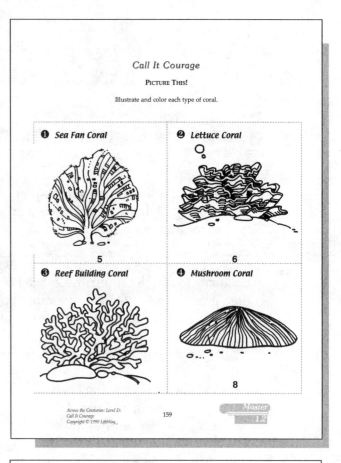

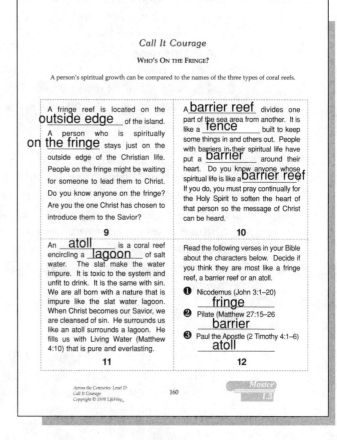

LESSON 2 (CHAPTER 2): THE SEA

1 Select a vocabulary activity for Lesson 2.

2 Refer students to Vocabulary Activity 3 to add information to their Captain's Sea Logs.

3 Assign each student a buddy reader and have them read Chapter 2, "The Sea."

4 Ask a student to read aloud the first sentence in Chapter 2.

1) Several students should describe in their own words what the author envisioned as he wrote it. *(Answer should make some reference to endless water, giving the impression of being without any direction.)* Direct students to write their own interpretation of the sentence in their Captain's Sea Logs.

2) What kind of mood does this beginning sentence set for the rest of the chapter? *(a mood of loneliness, being forlorn, hopeless)*

3) What might Tavana Nui have thought when he discovered his son missing? *(Accept any reasonable answer.)*

4) Mafatu knew the world of the sea was ruled by nature's law of survival. What do you think that law means? *(The weak are destroyed. The strong survive.)*

5 Direct students to look up Job 38:8-11 and ask a student to read the passage aloud. Who really rules the world of the sea? *(God, the Creator of all things)*

6 Mafatu saw an octopus with tentacles 30 feet long. Choose a spacious area, outside if possible. From a central point representing the body of an octopus, direct students to measure and mark eight tentacles, each reaching 30 feet in length from the body.

7 Mafatu's canoe lost its sail and mast in the turbulent storm. He had no control or guidance, so he was swept along at the mercy of the ocean currents. Without Christ to guide our lives, how would we be like Mafatu and his wrecked canoe? *(We would be at the mercy of the world and its standards. We would be swept away by "currents" of false teaching. Christ is the One who knows the paths we must take in our lives. He guides us; all we really must do is trust and obey. Read Colossians 2:6-8.)*

8 Distribute copies of **Master 2.1**. Direct students to label the equator, tropic of Capricorn and tropic of Cancer on the map.

9 Discuss the progression of Mafatu's journey.

1) Mafatu noticed that the ocean current was moving him in a southwestern direction. When he first saw an island in the distance, he wondered if it might be Tahiti. Locate Tahiti on a map. If Mafatu was traveling southwest towards Tahiti, would it be more probable that his home of Hikueru was located in French Polynesia or Line Islands? *(French Polynesia. It is northeast of Tahiti.)*

2) Do you think Mafatu was alarmed when the current turned in a westward direction? *(Yes, the black islands, home of the eaters-of-men lie to the west.)*

3) What were the mysterious belts north and south of the equator? Mafatu knew them as the home of the hurricane. *(the tropic of Capricorn, the tropic of Cancer)*

10 Locate an informational video on hurricanes and tropical storms. Provide photographs of hurricanes taken from satellites. Discuss with students how the calm at the eye of a hurricane is surrounded by a wall of powerful rotating winds. How can that be compared to the supernatural peace we can experience as the powerful winds of life in this world blow all around us? *(When we are assured of Christ abiding in us, we know that His eyes never turn from us. This gives us a peace that is beyond human understanding. Accept any ideas students may express that reflect thought about the comparison.)*

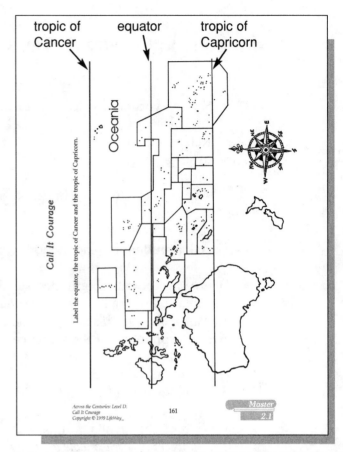

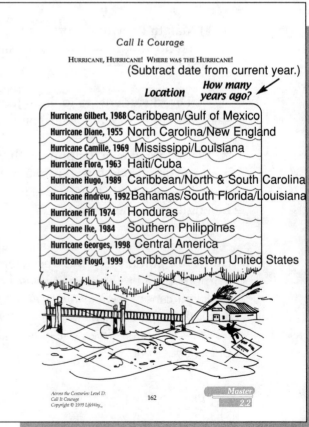

11 Provide an opportunity for enrichment or extra credit.

1) Distribute copies of **Master 2.2**. Instruct students to research where the listed hurricanes occurred. Use a hemisphere map for them to plot the path of selected hurricanes. (The National Hurricane Center in Coral Gables, Florida, can provide current information and instructional materials. Call (305) 666-4612.)

2) Make a geometric weaving to produce an abstract representation of the winds spiraling around the eye of a hurricane. See **Master 2.3**.

3) Distribute copies of **Master 2.4**. Allow students to use research materials as they fill in the blanks.

12 Use **Master 2.5** as an evaluation tool for Chapters 1 and 2.

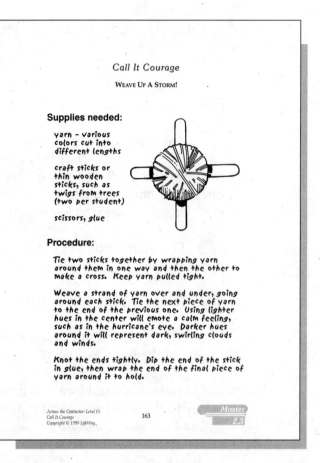

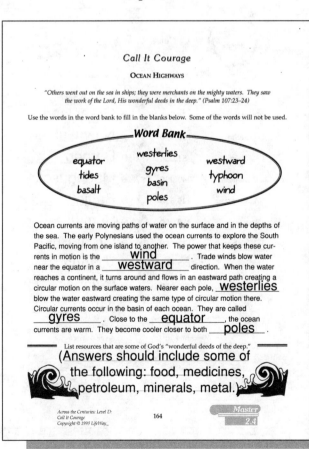

Lesson 3 (Chapter 3): The Island

1 Assign vocabulary activities to begin Lesson 3. Continue work on a class glossary as desired.

2 Ask students to list the descriptors of an island. *(mass of land, surrounded on all sides by water, smaller than a continent)* Write the following words on the board: island, atoll, Hawaii, Australia, United States, Alaska, Florida. Which ones are examples of islands? Which ones are non-examples? *(Examples: island, atoll, Hawaii. Non-examples: Australia, United States, Alaska, Florida)*

3 Distribute copies of **Master 3.1**. Discuss directions and assign it as independent work.

4 Read Chapter 3, "The Island," and use the following questions for discussion.

1) Whom did Mafatu credit with guiding him safely to the island? *(Maui, god of the fishermen)*

2) Students should locate Matthew 4:18-20 in their Bibles. What does Jesus say to the fishermen casting their nets into the Sea of Galilee? *("Follow Me, and I will make you fishers of men.")*

3) Ask students to use their Captain's Sea Log and explain the difference between Maui, god of the fishermen, and Jesus, a fisher of men. *(Maui, a pagan god, controls quality of catch according to islanders; Jesus and His "fishers of men" change lives.)* After they are finished writing their explanations, ask them to share their thoughts with a peer.

4) What does it mean to cauterize a wound? *(destroy infected tissue by burning or using a caustic agent such as limes)*

5 Read and discuss the description of Mafatu's trek up the trail that led through the foothills to a plateau. Direct students to illustrate and color in detail all that he observed as he climbed.

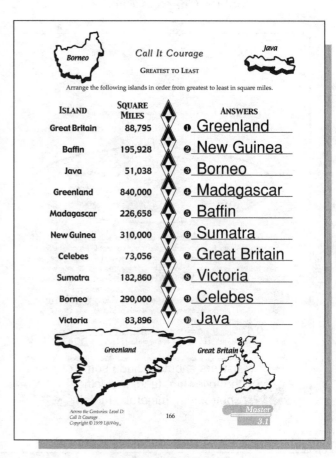

Across the Centuries: Level D: Call It Courage

6 Provide a snack day to sample some of the tropical fruits mentioned in this chapter. Ask students to bring samples to share. *(breadfruit, bananas, oranges, guavas, mangos, fresh pineapple, limes, coconuts)*

7 Students should be able to discern a change in Mafatu by the end of Chapter 3. How was his attitude different at this point in the story? What caused the change? *(more confident, less anxious about future; found the spear and took it from idol, recognized courage in himself)*

8 Mafatu found breadfruit growing on the island. The breadfruit was full of nutrients and vitamins. It aided in the restoration of Mafatu's strength. In the Bible, God provided bread for his people when they were in need. Use **Master 3.2** to enlighten students about God's provision.

9 Use a bread machine and allow the class to make and sample a whole grain bread. Use the recipe on **Master 3.3** or provide one of your personal favorites. Complete the math activity as a group.

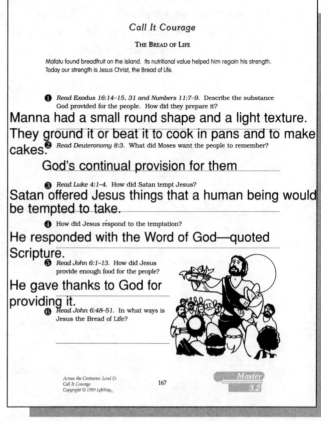

Call It Courage
THE BREAD OF LIFE

Mafatu found breadfruit on the island. Its nutritional value helped him regain his strength. Today our strength is Jesus Christ, the Bread of Life.

1 Read Exodus 16:14–15, 31 and Numbers 11:7-9. Describe the substance God provided for the people. How did they prepare it?
Manna had a small round shape and a light texture. They ground it or beat it to cook in pans and to make cakes.

2 Read Deuteronomy 8:3. What did Moses want the people to remember?
God's continual provision for them

3 Read Luke 4:1-4. How did Satan tempt Jesus?
Satan offered Jesus things that a human being would be tempted to take.

4 How did Jesus respond to the temptation?
He responded with the Word of God—quoted Scripture.

5 Read John 6:1-13. How did Jesus provide enough food for the people?
He gave thanks to God for providing it.

6 Read John 6:48-51. In what ways is Jesus the Bread of Life?

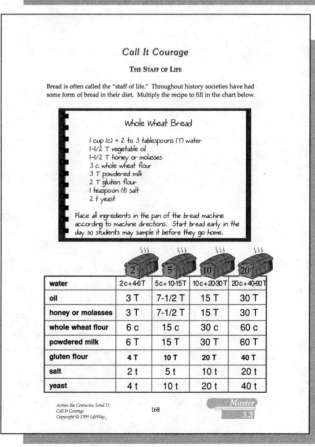

Call It Courage
THE STAFF OF LIFE

Bread is often called the "staff of life." Throughout history societies have had some form of bread in their diet. Multiply the recipe to fill in the chart below.

Whole Wheat Bread

1 cup (c) + 2 to 3 tablespoons (T) water
1-1/2 T vegetable oil
1-1/2 T honey or molasses
3 c whole wheat flour
3 T powdered milk
2 T gluten flour
1 teaspoon (t) salt
2 t yeast

Place all ingredients in the pan of the bread machine according to machine directions. Start bread early in the day so students may sample it before they go home.

	2	5	10	20
water	2c+4-6T	5c+10-15T	10c+20-30T	20c+40-60T
oil	3 T	7-1/2 T	15 T	30 T
honey or molasses	3 T	7-1/2 T	15 T	30 T
whole wheat flour	6 c	15 c	30 c	60 c
powdered milk	6 T	15 T	30 T	60 T
gluten flour	4 T	10 T	20 T	40 T
salt	2 t	5 t	10 t	20 t
yeast	4 t	10 t	20 t	40 t

10 Direct students to use the diagram on **Master 3.4** to compare Mafatu's home, Hikueru, with the physical features of the volcanic island.

11 Distribute copies of **Master 3.5** to be used as an evaluation tool.

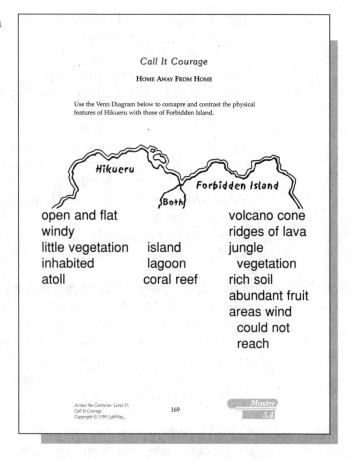

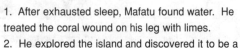

1. After exhausted sleep, Mafatu found water. He treated the coral wound on his leg with limes.
2. He explored the island and discovered it to be a Forbidden Island of "the eaters-of-men."
3. Mafatu realized his courage when he took a spear from the base of the pagan idol used for sacrifice.

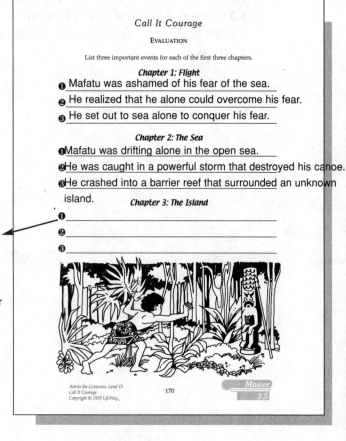

LESSON 4 (CHAPTER 4): THE DRUMS

1 Complete the class glossary by adding vocabulary words for Lessons 4 and 5.

2 Ask a student to read aloud the first two paragraphs of Chapter 4. As Christians, we know God will use any circumstance in our lives to our benefit, even the most difficult. Although Mafatu was not a Christian, how did difficult circumstances in his life prove to be beneficial? *(He could make tools, weapons and fishing nets. At home this was considered woman's work and was humiliating for him. He was glad to have the skills while stranded.)*

3 Read and discuss Chapter 4.

1) Direct a student to make a list on the board of the tasks Mafatu had to do to survive on the island, as well as plan his escape. *(build a canoe, make a fish trap, weave a fishing net, make a fishhook, make a bamboo raft)*

2) How did Mafatu make the decision of what to build first? *(raft; without it he could not fish)*

3) What qualities did Mafatu possess in order to be able to make his knife and adze? *(patience, perseverance, determination, instinct to survive)*

4) Where did Mafatu get the courage to attack the hammerhead shark? *(Uri was in danger.)*

4 Distribute copies of the math activity on **Master 4.1**.

5 Brainstorm ways the whale skeleton came to be in the sheltered cove. Encourage creative thinking. Make a list of ideas on the board or chart paper. Direct students to use their Captain's Sea Logs as they write a creative story about how the whale skeleton came to be in the hidden cove.

6 Choose a few students to take the role of Mafatu and dramatize the adventure of killing the wild boar.

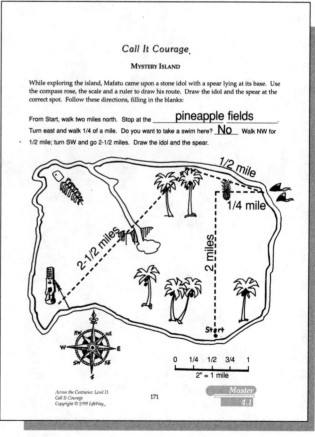

7 Direct students to build a *papier mache* model of the giant clam. Use the dimensions given to make it the actual size. Divide the class into small groups and instruct each group to write a brief paragraph on chart paper telling one or two facts about clams. Display the model clam and the charts in the hall and invite classes to come by and observe them.

8 To bring closure to the chapter, students may choose one event and illustrate it in detail on drawing paper. Display these story boards in the correct sequence. They can write one paragraph describing the action in the scene. Be sure each paragraph has a topic sentence and at least three supporting statements.

LESSON 5 (CHAPTER 5): HOMEWARD

1 Direct a review exercise for vocabulary, selecting an activity from the Preparation for Reading section.

2 Read and discuss Chapter 5.

3 Mafatu used his perfected sailing skills to put his vessel on one tack and then another. What, in sailing terms, does that mean? *(Tacking is a method used to sail to a destination that is upwind. The ship is steered in a series of courses, first to the left, then to the right to zigzag across the wind direction.)*

4 Allow students to demonstrate their own interpretation of a "measured booming" using their hands or a drum. Bring examples of island music to play during reading time.

5 Plan a day for students to display personal collections of shells, marine life and artifacts to class. Provide a conch shell for observation. Direct each student to prepare a brief presentation about his or her collection.

6 Direct students to locate the information needed from the chapter to solve the following question using mental math. How many warriors were in pursuit of Mafatu as he left Forbidden Island? *(60)*

7 Distribute copies of **Master 5.1** and direct students to write a short story using the story starter provided.

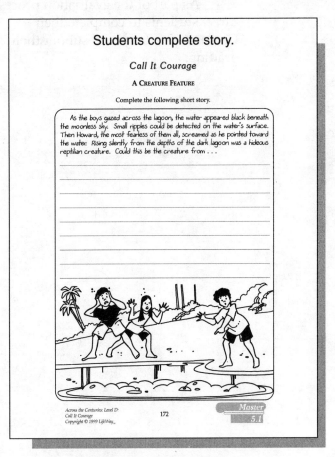

Across the Centuries: Level D:
Call It Courage

8 Read Luke 15:11–32 to the class. Ask students how they interpret the phrase, "unconditional love." Allow time to discuss the point, being certain everyone has an opportunity to contribute. Distribute copies of **Master 5.2** to be completed independently.

9 Direct half of the class to pretend they are Mafatu writing a letter to his father explaining why he must leave home. They can tear their letter around the edges to give it a ragged effect, put it in a plastic bottle and send it to someone in the other half of the class. Upon receiving the letter, students will be Mafatu's father answering his son's letter. Ask them to write in the letter what they would say if they (as Mafatu's father) would have acted like the father of the Prodigal Son (Luke 15:11-24).

10 Use **Master 5.3** as an evaluation tool.

11 As part of the evaluation process, direct students to complete their Captain's Sea Logs and submit them for grading.

Call It Courage
CONDITIONS OF LOVE

To have unconditional love for someone is to be able to love them just as Jesus does. That means to love them even if they do something wrong. Jesus' love is constant, total and complete.

1. allowed him to leave with his portion of goods, watched for his return and ran to meet him, welcomed him with compassion, prepared a celebration in his honor

2. respect for his father, accepting responsibility for his own weakness, a desire to bring honor to his father and his people

3. No, Mafatu is an embarrassment to his father because of his fear of the sea.

4. Some possible answers: pray for them, do not be easily angered, be quick to forgive, encourage them.

Master 5.2

Call It Courage
THE NEW MAFATU

MAFATU

	His Fears	His Reasons	His Victories
❶	the sea	lost at sea; mother died	completed sea voyage
❷	stone idol	eaters-of-men sacrificed there	took a spear
❸	hammerhead shark	could kill him	killed shark
❹	dropped knife in sea	hidden sea creatures	retrieved knife, killed octopus
❺	wild boar	powerful animal, hard to kill	killed boar, made necklace of tusks
❻	eaters-of-men	warriors; made human sacrifices	outran them in his canoe

Master 5.3

ENRICHMENT

1. Read Jules Verne's novel, *20,000 Leagues Under the Sea*, to the class.

2. Read excerpts from *Kon-Tiki* by Thor Heyerdahl, an account of his expedition across the Pacific Ocean from Peru to Polynesia on a balsa raft in 1947. Students will especially enjoy the Special Rand McNally Color Edition for Young People.

3. Direct students to prepare a notebook on Easter Island. Have students include pictures, drawings, historical information, facts about the culture and other information they deem interesting. Have students carve the mysterious statues of Easter Island using bars of soap.

4. Encourage students to develop a historical study of the Hawaiian Islands and/or the Florida Keys.

5. Invite an expert in deep sea diving to bring scuba gear and give a demonstration of how this equipment is used.

6. Plan a shipwreck museum in your classroom. Students can research famous historical shipwrecks. They can develop murals of the sea and construct examples of wreckage and articles recovered from the sea.

7. Visit a local aquarium or shipwreck museum.

8. Read to the class the Caldecott Medal winner for 1946, *The Little Island*, by Golden MacDonald and illustrated by Leonard Weisgard. Discuss with students the significance of the Caldecott Medal as it is awarded to illustrators of children's literature. Present each picture to the class and discuss in detail the art techniques they observe. Notice line, shading, perspective, color hues and values, proportions on the page and dimension.

9. Instruct students to choose a landform such as a hill, river, plain, mountain, plateau, mesa, lake, ocean or island, and find illustrations and information about what plant and animal life might be found inhabiting the area. Have them illustrate in detail and color the landform habitat and write a brief text about each illustration. Use *The Little Island* as a pattern book. This activity will allow artistic students to share their special gifts with others. Ask the school librarian if the students' pictures may be displayed in the library for others to enjoy.

10. Announce that the class has become a South Pacific travel agency and must fill the room with travel posters. Bring examples of travel posters to show and discuss as models for the students as they complete the assignment.

11 Web sites to try:

National Weather Service, Tropical Prediction Center:
http://www.nhc.noaa.gov/

The Weather Underground: wunderground.com:80/tropical

http://www.ncstormtrack.com/

http://www.hurricane.weathercenter.com/

Call It Courage

Captain's Sea Log

Date

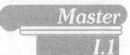

Across the Centuries: Level D:
Call It Courage
Copyright © 1999 LifeWay™

157

Master
1.1

Call It Courage

CORAL AND CORAL REEFS

Search the library, CD-ROMS and the Internet for the answers to the following questions. Proofread your work for punctuation, spelling, neatness, complete sentences and accuracy.

❶ What is coral?

❷ What are individual coral animals called?

❸ How do polyps form a coral colony?

❹ How do coral reefs form?

❺ What are the two main kinds of coelenterates (the group of sea animals to which corals belong)?

❻ Draw a coral polyp and label its parts: foot, calcium cup, opening, tentacles with stingers.

❼ Name the three main kinds of coral reefs.

❽ Study the drawings and find pictures in research materials to match. Label each type of reef.

_____

_____

_____

Call It Courage

PICTURE THIS!

Illustrate and color each type of coral.

❶ **Sea Fan Coral**	❷ **Lettuce Coral**
5	6
❸ **Reef Building Coral**	❹ **Mushroom Coral**
7	8

Across the Centuries: Level D:
Call It Courage
Copyright © 1999 LifeWay™

Master 1.2

Call It Courage

WHO'S ON THE FRINGE?

A person's spiritual growth can be compared to the names of the three types of coral reefs.

A fringe reef is located on the _____ of the island. A person who is spiritually _____ stays just on the outside edge of the Christian life. People on the fringe might be waiting for someone to lead them to Christ. Do you know anyone on the fringe? Are you the one Christ has chosen to introduce them to the Savior?

9

A _____ divides one part of the sea area from another. It is like a _____ built to keep some things in and others out. People with barriers in their spiritual life have put a _____ around their heart. Do you know anyone whose spiritual life is like a _____? If you do, you must pray continually for the Holy Spirit to soften the heart of that person so the message of Christ can be heard.

10

An _____ is a coral reef encircling a _____ of salt water. The salt makes the water impure. It is toxic to the system and unfit to drink. It is the same with sin. We are all born with a nature that is impure like the salt water lagoon. When Christ becomes our Savior, we are cleansed of sin. He surrounds us like an atoll surrounds a lagoon. He fills us with Living Water (Matthew 4:10) that is pure and everlasting.

11

Read the following verses in your Bible about the characters below. Decide if you think they are most like a fringe reef, a barrier reef or an atoll.

❶ Nicodemus (John 3:1–20)
_____

❷ Pilate (Matthew 27:15–26
_____

❸ Paul the Apostle (2 Timothy 4:1–6)
_____

12

Call It Courage

Label the equator, the tropic of Cancer and the tropic of Capricorn.

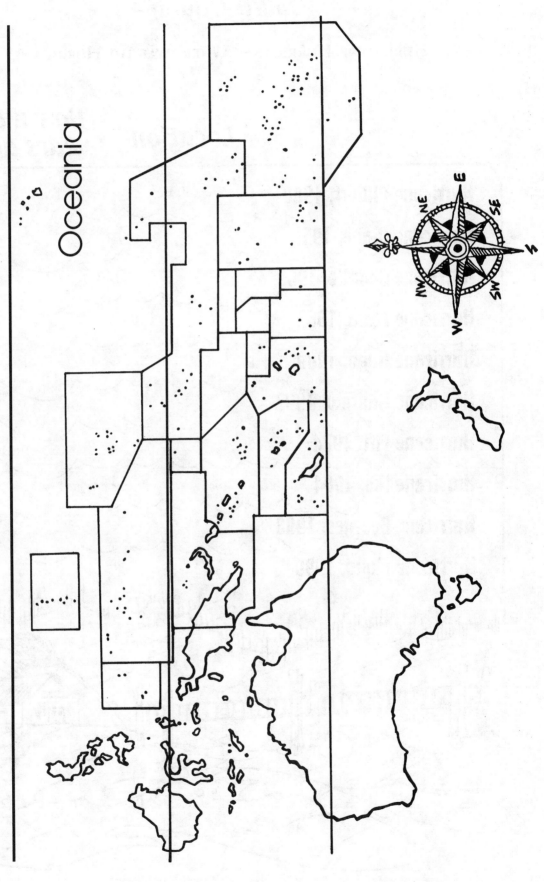

Across the Centuries: Level D:
Call It Courage
Copyright © 1999 LifeWay™

161

Master
2.1

Call It Courage

Hurricane, Hurricane! Where was the Hurricane!

Location   **How many years ago?**

- Hurricane Gilbert, 1988
- Hurricane Diane, 1955
- Hurricane Camille, 1969
- Hurricane Flora, 1963
- Hurricane Hugo, 1989
- Hurricane Andrew, 1992
- Hurricane Fifi, 1974
- Hurricane Ike, 1984
- Hurricane Georges, 1998
- Hurricane Floyd, 1999

Call It Courage

Weave Up A Storm!

Supplies needed:

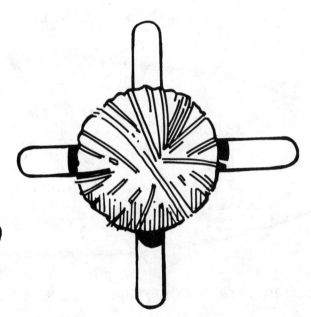

yarn - various colors cut into different lengths

craft sticks or thin wooden sticks, such as twigs from trees (two per student)

scissors, glue

Procedure:

Tie two sticks together by wrapping yarn around them in one way and then the other to make a cross. Keep yarn pulled tight.

Weave a strand of yarn over and under, going around each stick. Tie the next piece of yarn to the end of the previous one. Using lighter hues in the center will emote a calm feeling, such as in the hurricane's eye. Darker hues around it will represent dark, swirling clouds and winds.

Knot the ends tightly. Dip the end of the stick in glue, then wrap the end of the final piece of yarn around it to hold.

Across the Centuries: Level D:
Call It Courage
Copyright © 1999 LifeWay™

Call It Courage

OCEAN HIGHWAYS

"Others went out on the sea in ships; they were merchants on the mighty waters. They saw the work of the Lord, His wonderful deeds in the deep." (Psalm 107:23–24)

Use the words in the word bank to fill in the blanks below. Some of the words will not be used.

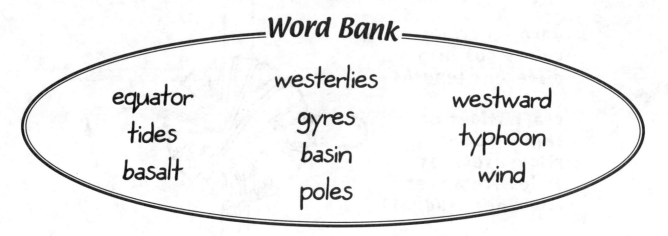

Word Bank: equator, tides, basalt, westerlies, gyres, basin, poles, westward, typhoon, wind

Ocean currents are moving paths of water on the surface and in the depths of the sea. The early Polynesians used the ocean currents to explore the South Pacific, moving from one island to another. The power that keeps these currents in motion is the _____ . Trade winds blow water near the equator in a _____ direction. When the water reaches a continent, it turns around and flows in an eastward path creating a circular motion on the surface waters. Nearer each pole, _____ blow the water eastward creating the same type of circular motion there. Circular currents occur in the basin of each ocean. They are called _____ . Close to the _____, the ocean currents are warm. They become cooler closer to both _____ .

List resources that are some of God's "wonderful deeds of the deep."

_____

_____

Across the Centuries: Level D:
Call It Courage
Copyright © 1999 LifeWay

Call It Courage

QUIZZLER

Answer the questions below for Chapters 1 and 2.

❶ Why was Mafatu known as the Boy Who Was Afraid
_____

❷ What did his name, Mafatu, actually mean
_____

❸ Why did Mafatu feel such compassion for Kivi
_____

❹ How did Kivi show his loyalty to Mafatu
_____

❺ Describe what it was like to be adrift in the open sea under the blazing sun
_____

❻ Do you think Uri was a good companion Explain your answer
_____

❼ As his craft came close to the island, what made Mafatu powerless to guide it
_____

❽ Describe how Mafatu reached the shore of the island
_____

❾ After reaching the island, what was Mafatu's most immediate need
_____

❿ What is the Southern Cross
_____

Call It Courage

Greatest to Least

Arrange the following islands in order from greatest to least in square miles.

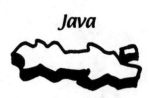

Island	Square Miles		Answers
Great Britain	88,795		❶ _____
Baffin	195,928		❷ _____
Java	51,038		❸ _____
Greenland	840,000		❹ _____
Madagascar	226,658		❺ _____
New Guinea	310,000		❻ _____
Celebes	73,056		❼ _____
Sumatra	182,860		❽ _____
Borneo	290,000		❾ _____
Victoria	83,896		❿ _____

Across the Centuries: Level D: Call It Courage
Copyright © 1999 LifeWay

Master 3.1

Call It Courage

THE BREAD OF LIFE

Mafatu found breadfruit on the island. Its nutritional value helped him regain his strength. Today our strength is Jesus Christ, the Bread of Life.

❶ *Read Exodus 16:14–15, 31 and Numbers 11:7–9.* Describe the substance God provided for the people. How did they prepare it?

_____

❷ *Read Deuteronomy 8:3.* What did Moses want the people to remember?

_____

❸ *Read Luke 4:1–4.* How did Satan tempt Jesus?

_____

❹ How did Jesus respond to the temptation?

_____

❺ *Read John 6:1–13.* How did Jesus provide enough food for the people?

_____

❻ *Read John 6:48–51.* In what ways is Jesus the Bread of Life?

_____

Across the Centuries: Level D:
Call It Courage
Copyright © 1999 LifeWay™

Master 3.2

Call It Courage

THE STAFF OF LIFE

Bread is often called the "staff of life." Throughout history societies have had some form of bread in their diet. Multiply the recipe to fill in the chart below.

Whole Wheat Bread

1 cup (c) + 2 to 3 tablespoons (T) water
1-1/2 T vegetable oil
1-1/2 T honey or molasses
3 c whole wheat flour
3 T powdered milk
2 T gluten flour
1 teaspoon (t) salt
2 t yeast

Place all ingredients in the pan of the bread machine according to machine directions. Start bread early in the day so students may sample it before they go home.

	2	5	10	20
water				
oil				
honey or molasses				
whole wheat flour				
powdered milk				
gluten flour	4 T	10 T	20 T	40 T
salt				
yeast				

Across the Centuries: Level D:
Call It Courage
Copyright © 1999 LifeWay

Master 3.3

Call It Courage

Home Away From Home

Use the Venn Diagram below to compare and contrast the physical features of Hikueru with those of Forbidden Island.

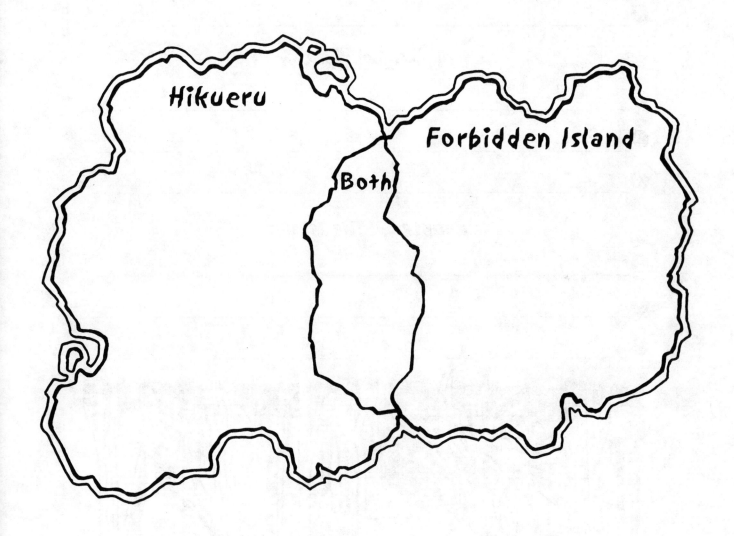

Call It Courage

EVALUATION

List three important events for each of the first three chapters.

Chapter 1: Flight

1. _____
2. _____
3. _____

Chapter 2: The Sea

1. _____
2. _____
3. _____

Chapter 3: The Island

1. _____
2. _____
3. _____

Call It Courage

MYSTERY ISLAND

While exploring the island, Mafatu came upon a stone idol with a spear lying at its base. Use the compass rose, the scale and a ruler to draw his route. Draw the idol and the spear at the correct spot. Follow these directions, filling in the blanks:

From Start, walk two miles north. Stop at the _____ _____. Turn east and walk 1/4 of a mile. Do you want to take a swim here? _____ Walk NW for 1/2 mile; turn SW and go 2-1/2 miles. Draw the idol and the spear.

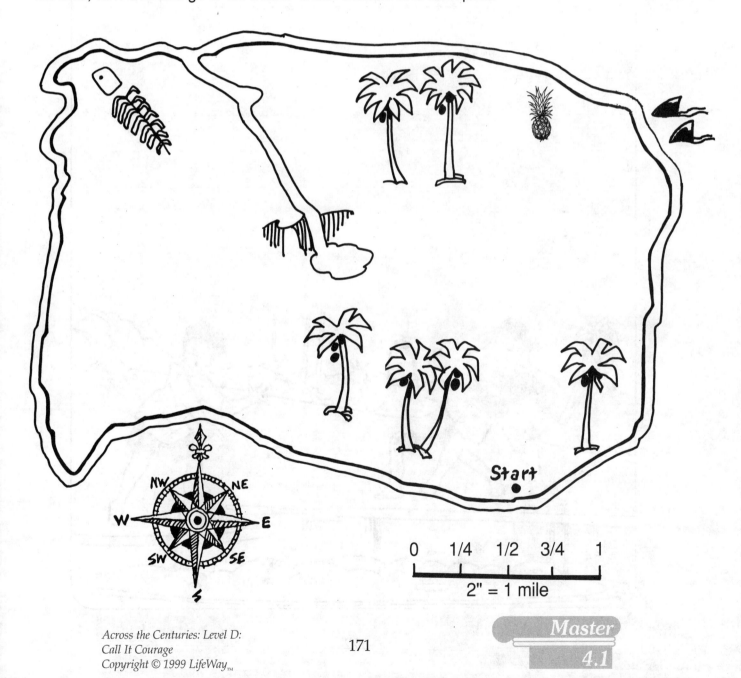

Call It Courage

A Creature Feature

Complete the following short story.

> As the kids gazed across the lagoon, the water appeared black beneath the moonless sky. Small ripples could be detected on the water's surface. Then Howard, the most fearless of them all, screamed as he pointed toward the water. Rising silently from the depths of the dark lagoon was a hideous reptilian creature. Could this be the creature from . . .

Call It Courage

CONDITIONS OF LOVE

To have unconditional love for others is to be able to love them just as Jesus does. That means to love them even if they do something wrong. Jesus' love is constant, total and complete.

❶ List ways the father in the Parable of the Lost Son, Luke 15:11–32, expressed unconditional love for his wayward son.

_____
_____
_____

❷ What character qualities do you see in Mafatu that you do not see in the son at the beginning of the parable?

_____
_____
_____

❸ Does Mafatu's father appear to express unconditional love for his son? Explain your answer.

_____
_____
_____

❹ In what ways can you express unconditional love toward your friends, and toward those who do not seem to be your friends?

_____
_____
_____
_____
_____
_____

Call It Courage

THE NEW MAFATU

MAFATU

	His Fears	His Reasons	His Victories
❶	the sea		
❷	stone idol		
❸	hammerhead shark		
❹	dropped knife in sea		
❺	wild boar		
❻	eaters-of-men		

Across the Centuries: Level D: Call It Courage Copyright © 1999 LifeWay™

Master 5.3

Across the Centuries

Volumes for this series now available:

Volume I

Level A – Preschool/Kindergarten

Brown Bear, Brown Bear, What Do You See?
The Mitten
Eating the Alphabet
The Doorbell Rang
The Cat in the Hat

Level B – Grades 1 & 2

Ira Sleeps Over
The Snowy Day
Ox-Cart Man
The Hundred Penny Box
Little House in the Big Woods

Level C – Grades 3 & 4

The Lion, the Witch, and the Wardrobe
Stone Fox
Homer Price
Misty

Level D – Grades 5 & 6

The Door in the Wall
Amos Fortune: Free Man
Caddie Woodlawn
Island of the Blue Dolphins

Level E – Grades 7 & 8

The Bronze Bow
Anne Frank: The Diary of a Young Girl
Treasure Island
Anne of Green Gables

Volume II

Level B – Grades 1 & 2

The Tale of Peter Rabbit
The Dragon-Fly (poem)
Owl Moon
Amelia Bedelia
The Birthday Child (poem)
The Runaway Bunny
Chrysanthemum

Level C – Grades 3 & 4

Helen Keller
The Family Under the Bridge
Jim Thorpe: Olympic Champion
Sarah, Plain and Tall

Level E – Grades 7 & 8

Sounder
The Poems of Robert Frost
The Prince and the Pauper
Across Five Aprils

To order additional volumes please contact LifeWay Christian School Resources (800) 458-2772.